TROLL

YOUNG PEOPLE'S
DICTIONARY

Library of Congress Cataloging-in-Publication Data

Smith, David, (date)
    Troll young people's dictionary / by David Smith and Derek Newton;
revised by Evelyn Goldsmith; illustrated by Clifford Bayly.
        p.   cm.
    Summary: A dictionary for primary grades explaining the meaning
and usage of words familiar to this age group.
    ISBN 0-8167-2255-2 (lib. bdg.) ISBN 0-8167-2256-0 (pbk.)
    1. English language—Dictionaries, Juvenile.   [1. English
language—Dictionaries.]   I. Newton, Derek.   II. Goldsmith, Evelyn.
III. Bayly, Clifford, ill.   IV. Title.
PE1628.5.S6 1990
423—dc20   89-27331

Published in the U.S.A. by Troll Associates, Inc.,
Produced for Troll Associates, Inc., by
Joshua Morris Publishing Inc. in association
with Harper Collins.
Copyright © 1991 by Harper Collins.
All rights reserved.
Printed in the U.S.A.
10 9 8 7 6 5 4 3 2

TROLL
YOUNG PEOPLE'S
DICTIONARY

by
David Smith and Derek Newton
Illustrated by Clifford Bayly
Revised by Evelyn Goldsmith

Troll Associates

How To Use This Book

You can use this book in three ways: to find out how to spell a word, to see what a word means, or to learn how to say a word.

The words in this dictionary are listed alphabetically. That means you should look up a word by turning to the section of words all starting with your word's first letter. The second and third letters of the word you're looking up decide its order in the section.

For example, suppose you want to look up the word **soil**. First turn to the section of words beginning with the letter **s**. The first word in this section is **sad** (top of page 99). Then move to the next letter. The second letter of **soil** is **o**, so now you have to go as far as the **so** words. The first **so** word is **soap** (bottom of page 105). The third letter of **soil** is **i**, so you will find **soil** after **soft** and before **soldier** (top of page 106). That is because **i** is between **f** and **l**. Try finding **sheep**, **bicycle**, and **prehistoric**.

The meaning of a word is called a definition. Sometimes a word has more than one definition, as **soil** does. It is usually quite easy to decide which definition you need. Sample sentences are often given to help you decide, and these are printed in italics. Beside the second definition of **soil**, for example, you'll find: *Playing in the garden might soil your clothes.*

Many of the words in this dictionary have pictures. These will help you understand the words they go with. Sometimes seeing a picture will make a word clearer in meaning for you.

A Guide for Saying a Word

Sometimes you will know what a word means but not know how to say it. That is why all the words in this dictionary have spellings next to them in parentheses to help you sound out the word. Most of these spellings are different from the correct spellings of the words. The reason is to make saying the word easier for you. The spellings in parentheses are also broken into parts called syllables, and the stronger syllables are printed in capital letters. In some cases, especially where two different words have the same spelling but are not said the same way, a rhyme has been added in the parentheses for each word.

If you are still not sure how to say a word correctly, ask a teacher, librarian, parent, or another adult. Remember that you are not alone —everyone has had trouble saying a word at one time or another. People will think more, not less, highly of you when you ask about a word because they will know you want to get it right. And that is what this dictionary will help you do—get words *right*.

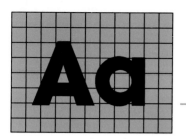

Aa

able (A-buhl)
having the skill or power to do something.

accident (AK-suh-DENT)
something, usually bad, that happens by chance.

accident

ache (aik)
a lasting, dull pain, such as a toothache.

act (akt)
1. to do something. *He had to act quickly to catch the thief.*
2. to pretend; to play a part. *John likes to act in the school play.*
3. a law passed by a government.
4. a part of a stage play.
5. something done.

active (AK-tiv)
full of life; busy.

add (ad)
to put together to make more. *If you add 2 to 4, you get 6.*

add

address (1. uh-DRES, AD-res; 2. uh-DRES)
1. the place where someone lives.
2. to speak to.

adult (uh-DULT, AD-ult)
a grown-up person or animal.

adventure (ad-VEN-chur)
an exciting or dangerous happening. *Jenny's trip to Disneyland was an adventure.*

afford (uh-FORD)
to have enough money to buy something. *Can you afford to buy that new toy?*

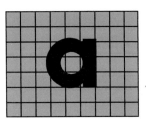

afraid (uh-FRAID)
frightened; full of fear.

afternoon (AF-tur-NOON)
the time between noon and evening.

against (uh-GENST)
1. leaning on; next to. *The ladder was against the wall.*
2. opposite to; facing someone or something, such as
   in a contest or battle.

against

age (aij)
1. the number of years someone has lived.
2. a special time in history, such as the Stone Age.

agree (uh-GREE)
to think or be willing to act the same as
   someone else.

aim (aim)
1. to point at something with a weapon. *You
   must aim carefully to be sure to hit the target.*
2. the act of pointing a weapon at something. *His
   aim was poor.*
3. a goal; to work toward a goal.

air (air)
the mix of gases we can't see or smell but still
   breathe every day.

airplane (AIR-plain)
a flying object with wings that is made by people and
   is heavier than air.

airplane

airport (AIR-port)
a place for airplanes and other flying machines to
   land and take off.

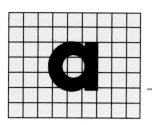

alarm (uh-LARM)
1. a warning. *The people went outside when the fire alarm sounded.*
2. to frighten. *Any loud noise can alarm Ken.*

alive (uh-LIVE)
living; not dead.

alligator (AL-uh-GAY-tur)
a large reptile with sharp teeth and a strong jaw that lives in China and the southeastern United States.

alligator

allow (uh-LOU; rhymes with "cow")
to give permission to let something be done.

alone (uh-LOHN)
all by yourself, with nobody else.

aloud (uh-LOUD)
able to be heard. *The teacher read aloud to her class.*

alphabet (AL-fuh-BET)
all the letters in a language put in a special order. *The English alphabet has twenty-six letters.*

amphibian (am-FIB-ee-un)
a cold-blooded animal such as a frog, toad, or salamander that often lives and lays its eggs in water.

amphibian

ancient (AIN-shunt)
very old; of times long ago.

angle (ANG-gul)
the shape made by two lines that meet.

angry (ANG-gree)
in a bad mood; very annoyed.

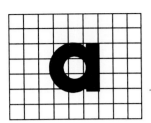

animal (AN-uh-mul)
anything living that is not a plant. *An animal can be a bird, fish, insect, reptile, or mammal.*

annoy (uh-NOY)
to tease and make someone angry.

answer (AN-sur)
what we say or write when we are asked a question.

ant (ant)
a busy, small insect of red or black color.

ant

antenna (an-TEN-uh)
1. a metal rod or wire used to help send or pick up radio or television signals.
2. one of the two wirelike body parts found on the head of an insect.

antler (ANT-lur)
a branchlike horn on a male deer, elk, or moose.

ape (ape)
a large, monkeylike animal without a tail.
A chimpanzee is an ape, and a gorilla is an ape.

ape

apple (AP-ul)
a round fruit that grows on a tree; it has a red, green, or yellow skin.

April (A-prul)
the fourth month of the year; it has thirty days.

aquarium (uh-KWAIR-ee-um)
a water-filled tank or container, usually with glass sides, where water plants, fish, and other water animals are kept.

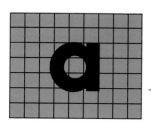

arch (arch)
1. the curved top of a door, bridge, or window.
2. to curve a part of the body. *I saw the cat arch its back.*

area (AIR-ee-uh)
1. the size of a flat surface. *The area of the floor was nine square yards.*
2. part of the earth's surface. *Oranges are grown in one area of California.*

argue (AR-gyoo)
to talk for or against something with a person who thinks differently; to give your reasons for something.

arm (arm)
1. the part of the body between the hand and shoulder.
2. to give someone a weapon.

armor (AR-mur)
a covering, usually of metal, worn to protect the body when fighting.

army (AR-mee)
1. a large group of people or other creatures.
2. a large number of people trained for war.

arrange (uh-RAINJ)
1. to put in some kind of order. *She will arrange the books alphabetically.*
2. to plan. *He will arrange the vacation.*

arrive (uh-RIVE)
to reach the place where you are going. *Chris will arrive at seven o'clock.*

arrow (AHR-roh)
a stick with a sharp tip that is shot from a bow.

arch

armor

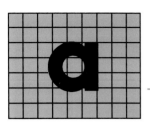

art (art)
1. a drawing, painting, or sculpture; also, music, poetry, and plays.
2. a special skill.

ash (ash)
1. what is left after something has been burned.
2. a kind of tree.

ash

ask (ask)
to question someone. *"If you need help, just ask," said the teacher in class.*

asleep (uh-SLEEP)
not awake; resting with your eyes closed and not knowing what is going on around you.

atlas (AT-lus)
a book of maps.

attack (uh-TAK)
to start a fight. *Cats attack mice.*

attention (uh-TEN-shun)
1. careful listening or watching.
2. the act of standing straight with your feet together and hands by your sides.

attack

audience (AW-dee-uns)
one or more people watching or listening to a play, a movie, or a talk.

August (AW-gust)
the eighth month of the year; it has thirty-one days.

awake (uh-WAYK)
not asleep; open-eyed and alert.

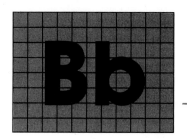

baby (BAY-bee)
a very young person or other creature.

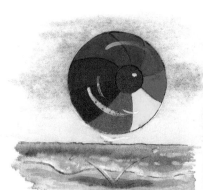
baby

back (bak)
1. the upper or rear part of the body where the spine is. *Tony had a ride on the back of a horse.*
2. the part of something opposite the front. *The back of the house was painted red.*
3. in return. *Sally paid back the money she owed.*

bad (bad)
1. not good.
2. spoiled.

badge (baj)
a sign usually worn to show that a person belongs to a school, group, or club. *The police officer wears a badge on his shirt.*

bag (bag)
a container made of thin material, such as paper or cloth, that is used to carry or hold things.

bake (bayk)
1. to cook food in an oven.
2. to make something by first making it hot. *The clay bricks must bake in the sun.*

balance (BAL-uns)
to keep steady. *A bird can balance itself while sitting on a wire.*

bald (bawld)
having no hair.

ball (bawl)
anything round, such as an orange.

ball

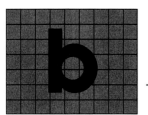

balloon (buh-LOON)
1. a small, thin rubber bag that can be blown up with the mouth and then tied off. *Toni held her balloon by a string.*
2. a very large bag that rises and floats when it's filled with hot air or a gas lighter than air. *The balloon had a big basket under it for carrying people into the air.*

banana (buh-NAN-uh)
a long, curved fruit with a yellow skin.

bananas

band (band)
1. a number of people who play music together.
2. a thin, narrow piece of material that fits around something. *John wears a band on his wrist when he plays tennis.*

bandage (BAN-dij)
1. a thin piece of cloth used to cover and tie up a wound.
2. to wrap up an injury.

bank (bangk)
1. a building where people keep their money safe.
2. the sloping ground at the river's edge.

bare (bair)
not covered; with nothing on. *The child's bare feet were cold.*

bark (bark)
1. the cry of a dog.
2. the outside covering of tree trunks and branches.

barn (barn)
a large building where a farmer stores hay, grain, and other crops, or where farm animals sleep.

barn

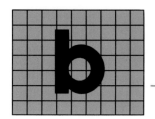

base (base)
1. the bottom of something; the part on which something stands or is built.
2. the square cloth bag used in baseball and softball games. *Leslie slid into second base.*

baseball (BASE-bawl)
a game played with a ball, bat, and nine players on each team.

basket (BAS-kit)
a container usually made from thin pieces of wood or straw that is used for carrying or holding things.

basketball (BAS-kit-bawl)
a game in which two teams of five players each try to throw a large ball through hoops above the ground.

bat (bat)
1. a piece of wood or metal used to hit a ball in some games.
2. a mouselike animal with wings that flies at night and rests by day.

bat

bathroom (BATH-room)
the room where the toilet and bathtub or shower are.

bathtub (BATH-tuhb)
a large container in which you wash your whole body.

battery (BAT-ur-ree)
a container for storing electricity. *Jack needs a new battery for his radio.*

battery

battle (BAT-ul)
a fight between armies, ships, or airplanes during a war.

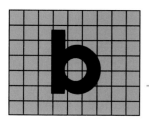

bay (bay)
water partly surrounded by land but
  that opens toward the sea.

beach (beech)
the sand or pebbles at the edge of an ocean or a lake.

beak (beek)
the hard, pointed or curved part of a bird's mouth.

bean (been)
a vegetable with large seeds that grow in pods.

bear (bair)
a large, heavy animal with thick fur that can stand
  on two feet.

beard (beerd)
the hair growing on a man's chin.

beautiful (BYOO-tuh-ful)
very pretty; very nice to see or hear.

beaver (BEE-vur)
a small, furry animal with a flat tail and webbed back
  feet that eats tree bark and builds dams.

bear

beaver

bed (bed)
1. something people sleep on, usually at night.
2. a place where plants are grown.
3. the bottom of an ocean, river, or lake.

bee (bee)
a flying insect that makes honey and wax.

beetle (BEE-tul)
an insect that has two hard wings covering and
  protecting its body.

bee

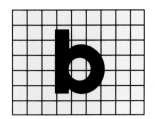

begin (bih-GIN)
to start. *The test will begin at nine o'clock.*

behave (bih-HAYV)
1. to act or to do. *Why do you behave like that?*
2. to be good in front of others. *Jill did behave herself at the concert.*

believe (bih-LEEV)
to think that something is true.

bell (bel)
a piece of metal shaped like an upside-down cup that makes a ringing sound when hit.

bell

belong (bih-LONG)
1. to be owned by someone. *Does this book belong to you?*
2. to be part of. *I belong to the club.*

belt (belt)
1. a long strip of material, such as leather, usually worn around the waist.
2. A strap for holding people or things. *Fasten your seat belt!*

bend (bend)
1. to make something curved or crooked. *You will have to bend the pipe to make it fit.*
2. the part of something that is curved or crooked. *Look out for the bend in the road.*

bicycle (BYE-si-kul)
a machine to ride, without a motor but with two wheels and two pedals to make the wheels turn.

bicycle

big (big)
large. *A blue whale is very big.*

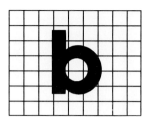

bird (burd)
an animal that has wings and feathers.

birthday (BURTH-day)
the day of the year when a person was born.

bite (bite)
to cut with the teeth. *The dog tried to bite the mailman.*

bird

blade (blaid)
the flat, sharp part of a tool.

blame (blaim)
1. to find fault with; to pick out whoever caused something to go wrong. *I blame the boys for breaking the window.*
2. responsibility for doing something wrong. *Sam and John must share the blame for the accident.*

blanket (BLANG-kit)
a thick cloth to keep warm in.

blind (blind)
1. not able to see.
2. a screen to keep out light. *Mother closed the blind when the sun was hot.*

blanket

block (blok)
1. a piece of hard material such as wood that has at least one flat side.
2. to be in the way of something. *My brother liked to block the door so I could not go in.*

blood (blud)
the red liquid in the body. *All people need blood to live.*

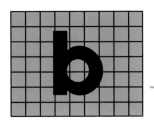

blow (bloh)
1. to send air out of the mouth. *Jack had to blow hard into the balloon.*
2. a hard knock or punch.

board (bord)
1. a long, flat piece of wood.
2. to get on a plane, boat, or train. *We will board the ferry tomorrow.*

boat

boat (boht)
a small ship; something hollow that floats and can carry people or things on water.

body (BOD-ee)
all the parts together of a person or other animal.

boil (boyl)
to heat water to the point where it bubbles and gives off steam.

bones (bohnz)
the hard frame inside the body that forms the skeleton.

bonfire

bonfire (BON-fire)
a fire lit outside. *They lit a bonfire on the beach.*

book (book)
pages of words, pictures, or both that are grouped together inside a cover. *Tim read at least one book a month.*

boot (boot)
a kind of shoe that covers part of the leg as well as the foot.

boot

bore (bor)
1. to make a hole in wood, metal, or other material.
2. to talk in a dull way.

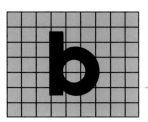

born (born)
brought into life. *Peter was born in Maine ten years ago.*

borrow (BAR-oh, BOR-oh)
to take something that will have to be given back. *May I borrow your pencil?*

bottle (BOT-ul)
a container for liquids. *The bottle is full of milk.*

bottle

bottom (BOT-um)
1. the lowest part. *The ship sank to the bottom of the ocean.*
2. the part of the body you sit on.

bounce (bouns)
to spring up and down. *See how many times the ball can bounce.*

bow (boh; rhymes with "so")
1. a knot with two loops used to tie ribbon or string.
2. a weapon used for shooting arrows.

bow (bou; rhymes with "now")
to stand and bend forward at the waist as a way of greeting someone.

bow

bowl (bohl)
1. a deep dish, usually round.
2. to play a game in which a ball is rolled and knocks over pins.

box (boks)
1. a container with straight sides. *Put your toys in the box.*
2. to fight with your fists.

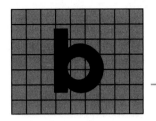

brain (brane)
body part inside the head that lets people and other
 animals think, learn, and remember; mind.

brake (brayk)
the part of a vehicle or any machine that slows it down
 or stops it. *Mr. Carter stepped hard on his car brake
 to avoid hitting the boy on the bicycle.*

brave (brayv)
not being afraid.

bread (bred)
a food made from flour and baked in an oven.

bread

break (brayk)
1. to crack or smash. *If you drop the eggs, they
 will break.*
2. a rest. *Let's take a break for half an hour.*

breakfast (BREK-fust)
the first meal of the day.

breath (breth)
the amount of air taken into the body and let out
 again.

breathe (breethe)
to take air into the body and let it out again.

brick

brick (brik)
a block, often of baked clay, used in building.

bridge (brij)
a way to cross over a river, road, or
 railway tracks.

bridge

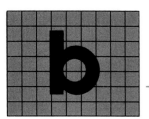

bright (brite)
1. shining; sending out light. *Jane covered her eyes because the sun was so bright.*
2. clever; smart. *She had always been bright in school.*

bring (bring)
to take along or carry something.

broom (broom)
a brush with a long handle.

bruise (brooz)
a mark on the skin caused by a bump or injury.

brush (brush)
a small tool made of many pieces of hair, straw, or plastic used for sweeping, cleaning, combing, or painting.

brush

bubble (BUB-ul)
1. a ball of liquid with air or gas inside.
2. to form bubbles. *Rubbing soap in water makes it bubble.*

bucket (BUK-it)
a round container with a handle for holding water or something else.

bucket

build (bild)
to make something; to put something together.

building (BIL-ding)
something that people make to shelter them, such as a house, store, or church.

building

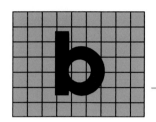

bulb (bulb)
1. a round plant root, often shaped like an onion, from which flowers grow. *A tulip grows from a bulb.*
2. the thin glass of an electric light.

bull (bul)
an adult male of animals such as seals, cattle, moose, whales, and elephants.

bump (bump)
1. to run into something or someone. *Sally will bump into the wall if she doesn't slow down.*
2. a swelling caused by an injury. *He fell and now has a bump on his head.*

bunch (bunch)
a group of things of the same kind, such as grapes.

bunch

bundle (BUN-dul)
several things tied or wrapped together.

burn (burn)
1. to be on fire. *The big log did not burn fast.*
2. to set fire to. *We will burn the paper first.*
3. an injury caused by heat or fire. *The child has a bad burn on his back.*

bus (bus)
a large vehicle for carrying passengers.

bus

busy (BIZ-ee)
having a lot to do. *The children are busy writing and drawing.*

butter (BUT-tur)
1. a soft, yellow food made from cream.
2. to spread this food on bread or pancakes. *Tommy likes to butter his bread.*

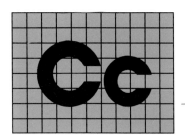

Cc

cactus (KAK-tus)
a plant covered with needles that grows in hot, dry areas.

cactus

cage (kayj)
a room or box that has wires or bars for keeping birds or other animals.

cake (kayk)
a sweet food made from flour, liquid, and eggs mixed together and baked.

cage

calculator (KAL-kyoo-LAY-tur)
a small machine used to add, subtract, multiply, and divide numbers.

calendar (KAL-un-dur)
a list of all the days and dates in each month of the year.

call (kawl)
1. to shout or cry out.
2. to telephone someone.
3. to give a name to someone or something. *We call him Ricky.*

camel (KAM-ul)
a large animal with either one or two humps on its back. *The camel is used to carry people and things in hot, dry lands.*

camera (KAM-ur-uh, KAM-ruh)
a machine used to take photographs.

camera

camp (kamp)
1. to live out of doors, often in a tent.
2. a place to stay where tents or very simple buildings are set up. *The scouts made their camp near a farm.*

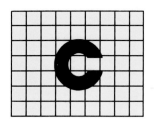

can (kan)
1. a metal container, often round.
2. to be able to. *Can you swim?*

candle (KAN-dul)
a stick of wax with a string in the middle that is burned
  to give light.

candle

candy (KAN-dee)
a sweet food made with a lot of sugar.

canoe (kuh-NOO)
a narrow, light boat with pointed ends that is moved
  with paddles.

canoe

cap (kap)
1. a small, soft hat worn closely on the head.
2. a lid.

capital (KAP-ih-tul)
1. the chief city of a country or state. *The capital of the
  United States is Washington, D.C.*
2. a large letter of the alphabet. *"A" is a capital and
  "a" is a small letter.*

captain (KAP-tun, KAP-tin)
1. the person in charge of a ship.
2. the leader of a team. *Bill is the football captain this
  year.*

capture (KAP-chur)
to take prisoner; to catch. *The police wanted to
  capture the bank robber.*

car (kar)
an automobile.

card (kard)
a small, flat piece of stiff paper.

car

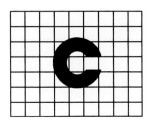

cardboard (KARD-bord)
a stiff, thick piece of paper used to make things such as boxes.

care (kayr)
1. paying attention to. *Take care when you cross the road.*
2. to look after. *If you are sick, someone will take care of you.*
3. to like someone or something. *I care very much for my brother.*

carnival (KAR-nih-vul)
a traveling show with games and rides.

carpet (KAR-pit)
a thick, heavy covering for the floor.

carry (KAIR-ee)
to pick up and take someone or something from one place to another.

carton (KAR-tun)
a box made of cardboard or plastic. *The eggs were packed in a carton.*

carry

cartoon (kar-TOON)
1. a kind of funny drawing.
2. a short, funny movie made with drawings.

castle (KAS-ul)
a building with thick stone walls and towers. *King Arthur rode back to his castle.*

castle

cat (kat)
a small, furry animal often kept as a pet that is good at catching mice and other small animals.

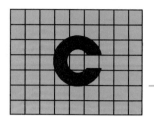

catch (kach)
1. to take hold of something that is moving. *Catch the ball with both hands.*
2. to find someone doing something wrong. *"Don't let me catch you walking on the train tracks!" said Fred's father.*
3. to chase people or animals and stop them. *I can catch my brother when he runs away.*

caterpillar (KAT-uh-PIL-ur, KAT-ur-PIL-ur)
a wormlike creature with many legs that turns into a butterfly or moth when it is an adult.

cattle (KAT-ul)
large animals with hooves and horns that are raised on ranches and farms.

cattle

cause (kawz)
1. why something happened. *Falling was the cause of his broken arm.*
2. an idea believed in and supported by many people. *Freedom is a cause worth fighting for.*

cave (kave)
a large hole under the ground with an opening to the surface.

ceiling (SEE-ling)
the inside roof of a room.

cave

center (SEN-tur)
the middle point.

centimeter (SEN-tih-MEE-tur)
a length equal to one hundredth of a meter, or 0.39 inch.

century (SEN-choo-ree)
one hundred years.

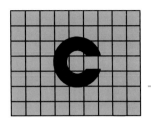

cereal (SEER-ee-ul)
a food made from grain and usually eaten
  at breakfast.

chair (chayr)
a single seat with legs and a back.

chalk (chawk)
a soft, white stone that is often used for writing on
  a blackboard.

chalk

chance (chans)
happening by accident or luck. *The two friends
  had met by chance at the baseball game.*

change (chaynj)
1. to make different. *New paint will change the color
  of the wall.*
2. money returned to someone who has paid
  too much. *Sarah got back fifty cents in change.*

channel (CHAN-ul)
1. a narrow stretch of water between two pieces
  of land.
2. one of many places on a television set where
  programs can be found. *Hank got up and
  changed the channel.*

chase (chays)
to run after.

chase

cheap (cheep)
costing only a little money.

check (chek)
1. to make sure something is right. *Will you check to
  see that the windows are shut?*
2. a special piece of paper used to get money from
  a bank.

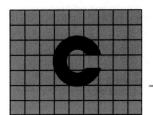

cheerful (CHEER-ful)
happy; glad.

cheese (cheez)
a solid food made from milk.

chest (chest)
1. a large, strong box with a lid.
2. the front part of the body between the waist and the
   neck.

chew (choo)
to crush and grind with the teeth.

chicken (CHIK-un, CHIK-in)
the most popular bird raised for eggs and meat.

chief

chief (cheef)
1. a leader. *The Indian chief spoke to the cowboys.*
2. most important. *The chief problem is too much
   noise.*

child (child)
a young boy or girl.

chimney (CHIM-nee)
an opening that leads to the outside and takes away
  smoke from a fire.

chimpanzee (CHIM-pan-ZEE)
an ape smaller than a gorilla.

chimpanzee

china (CHI-nuh)
dishes of all kinds made from a special, hard, white
  clay that has been baked.

chips (chips)
1. thin, hard slices of potato cooked in oil.
2. pieces cut or broken off of something.

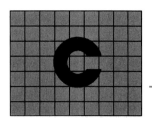

chocolate (CHA-ka-lit, CHOK-lit)
a sweet candy or drink made from cacao beans.

choose (chooz)
to pick out.

chop (chop)
to cut with a sharp tool. *Chop down that tree!*

church (church)
a building where people get together to pray.

church

circle (SUR-kul)
a perfectly round shape, like a ring.

circus (SUR-kus)
a traveling show held in a tent or building, with
  animals, clowns, and people doing amazing things.

city (SIT-ee)
a very large town.

clap (klap)
1. to slap the hands together. *Let's clap if we like the
  dancing.*
2. a sudden loud noise. *A clap of thunder made us
  all jump.*

class (klas)
a group of students who are taught together.

clay (klay)
soft, sticky earth used to make bricks and pottery.

clay

clean (kleen)
1. washed; without dirt.
2. to wash away the dirt from something.

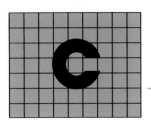

clear (kleer)
1. open; with nothing in the way. *The snow has been moved so the roads are now clear.*
2. easy to see through, such as a window.

clever (KLEV-ur)
being quick at learning.

cliff (klif)
a high, steep wall of rock.

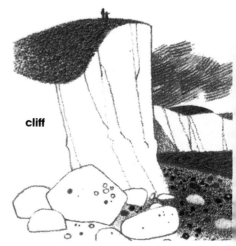

cliff

climate (KLY-mit)
the kind of weather a place has.

climb (klime)
to go up or down.

clock (klok)
a machine for telling time.

close (klohz; rhymes with "toes")
to shut. *Please close the door.*

close (klohs; rhymes with "dose")
near. *Mrs. Walsh parked the car close to the sidewalk.*

clocks

clothes (klohz, klohthz)
things people wear to cover their bodies.

cloud (kloud)
1. very many tiny drops of water and ice floating together in the sky.
2. a large amount of smoke, steam, or dust.

club (klub)
1. a heavy stick.
2. a group of people who meet to do things together.

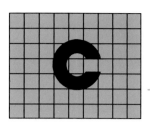

clumsy (KLUM-zee)
not moving smoothly or well. *Alan was clumsy and knocked over the radio.*

coach (kohch)
1. a person who trains or teaches, usually in sports.
2. to train or teach someone, usually in sports.

coal (kohl)
a kind of hard, black rock dug out of the ground that can be burned to give off heat.

coat (koht)
an outer covering. *Ann wore her coat because it was cold. The house needs a coat of paint. A sheep's coat is called a fleece.*

coat

cobweb (KOB-web)
a net made by a spider to trap insects.

cocoa (KOH-koh)
brown powder made from the fruit (beans) of the cacao tree.

coffee (KAW-fee)
a hot drink made from the roasted beans of the coffee plant.

coin (koin)
a piece of money made of metal.

coin

cold (kohld)
1. the opposite of hot. *Ice is cold.*
2. an illness of the nose and throat.

college (KOL-ij)
a place for learning, usually entered after high school.

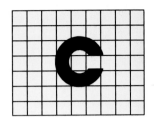

comfortable (KUM-fur-tuh-bul, KUMF-tuh-bul)
to be or feel relaxed; at rest.

common (KOM-un)
1. usual.
2. found in many places.
3. shared by two or more people. *Tom, Jan, and Sue have many interests in common.*

company (KUM-puh-nee)
1. a group of people working together to make or sell things.
2. someone or a group of people who come to visit.

compare (kum-PARE)
to see if things are alike or different.

compass (KUM-pus)
1. an instrument that can show east, west, north, and south.
2. an instrument for drawing circles.

compass

competition (KOM-pih-TISH-un)
a type of game where there will be a winner; a contest.

computer (kum-PYOO-tur)
a machine that can find, arrange, and give information quickly.

concentrate (KON-sun-TRATE)
to give all your attention to something.

container (kun-TAY-nur)
a box, can, jar, or pot used to hold something.

container

contest (KON-test)
a game or test where there will be a winner. *Paul won the spelling contest at school.*

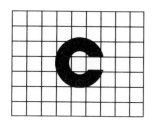

control (kun-TROL)
1. to make someone or something behave exactly as you want.
2. any part of a machine that makes the machine work in different ways.

cook (kuhk)
1. to heat food and get it ready for eating.
2. a person who gets meals ready.

cookie (KUHK-ee)
a small, sweet, usually flat cake.

cookies

cool (kool)
not warm but not very cold.

copper (KOP-ur)
a metal that is reddish in color.

copy (KOP-ee)
1. anything made exactly like something else.
2. to act the same as.

cord (kord)
1. threads or fibers twisted together.
2. the covered wire carrying electricity for a lamp or machine.

cork (kork)
1. a stopper for the opening of a bottle.
2. the light, thick bark of a kind of oak tree.

corn (korn)
a grain with yellow seeds growing in rows.

corn

corner (KOR-nur)
the place where two lines meet, or where two streets or walls meet.

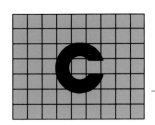

cost (kawst)
the price paid for something. *The cost of food keeps rising.*

cot (kot)
a small bed that can be folded up and is often used for camping.

cot

cotton (KOT-un)
cloth made from the soft, white seed covering of the cotton plant.

cough (kawf)
the noise made when air is sent suddenly out of the lungs. *We could hear Jim cough down the hall.*

count (kount)
1. to find out how many.
2. to say numbers in their correct order.

country (KUN-tree)
1. land far outside of towns and cities.
2. the land where a nation of people lives. *China is a country with a huge number of people.*

cover (KUV-ur)
1. to put something on a person or thing for protection.
2. anything that gives shelter.

cow (kow)
1. a large farm animal raised to give milk.
2. an adult female of such animals as elephants, whales, seals, cattle, and moose.

cowboy; cowgirl (KOU-boy; KOU-gurl)
a person who takes care of cattle or horses on a ranch.

cowboy

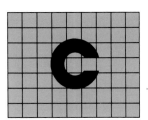

coyote (kye-OH-tee, KYE-oht)
a four-legged animal with a bushy tail that is related to
   wolves and dogs.

crab (krab)
a sea animal with a hard shell, eight legs, and two
   big claws.

crab

crack (krak)
1. a sharp noise. *There was a crack of thunder.*
2. a thin opening or split. *There is a crack in your cup.*

crane (krayn)
1. a machine for lifting large and heavy things.
2. a large water bird with long legs.

crash (krash)
1. a loud noise made by breaking.
2. an accident.
3. to hit against and be damaged. *Sally saw the car
   crash into the wall.*

crawl (krawl)
to move on hands and knees.

crayon

crayon (KRAY-on, KRAY-un)
a stick of colored wax used for drawing.

creature (KREE-chur)
any living animal, including a person. *Some creature
   tried to get into our house last night.*

crocodile (KROK-uh-DILE)
a reptile like an alligator but with a longer snout.

crooked (KROOK-id)
1. not straight; bent.
2. not to be trusted or believed. *He was a crooked
   salesman.*

crocodile

35

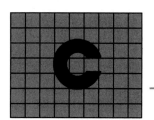

crop (krop)
a plant (often a food plant) grown in large numbers by
  people. *The wheat crop was bigger than ever.*

cross (kros)
1. a shape like "+" or "×."
2. angry.
3. to go from one side to another.

crowd (kroud)
a large number of people together in one place.

crowd

crush (krush)
to squeeze together.

crust (krust)
the hard, outside part of things such as bread, pies, or
  the earth.

cure (kyoor)
1. to make a sick person better.
2. to keep from spoiling. *The farmer put the bacon in
  the smokehouse to cure it.*

curl (kurl)
to roll up in a round shape.

curtain (KUR-tun, KUR-tin)
cloth that covers a window or a stage in the theater.

curve (kurv)
a line that bends gradually.

curve

cut (kut)
to make something into smaller pieces by using a
  knife, scissors, or a saw.

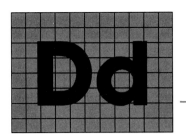

Dd

dam (dam)
a wall built to hold back water.

damage (DAM-ij)
to spoil or break something.

damp (damp)
slightly wet. *Her hair was still damp from the shower.*

dam

dance (dans)
to move your body in time to music.

dangerous (DANE-jur-us)
unsafe; likely to cause harm. *It is dangerous to skate on thin ice.*

dark (dark)
without light.

date (dayt)
1. the fruit of a palm tree.
2. the day, month, and year. *The date I was born was May 6, 1983.*

day (day)
1. the time between sunrise and sunset.
2. twenty-four hours.

date

dazzle (DAZ-ul)
to blind for a time with bright light.

deaf (def)
not able to hear.

dear (deer)
loved very much. *The child was dear to her family.*

death (deth)
the ending of life.

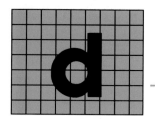

December (Dih-SEM-bur)
the twelfth month of the year; it has thirty-one days.

decide (dih-SIDE)
to make up your mind.

deep (deep)
a long way down; not shallow. *Parts of the ocean are very deep.*

deer (deer)
a quick-running, grass-eating animal with four long legs; the male, or buck, has antlers that look like branches.

deer

dent (dent)
a small bend in a smooth surface.

describe (dih-SKRIBE)
to give a picture of somebody or something in words or writing.

desert (DEZ-urt)
a hot, dry, sandy area with little rain.

deserve (dih-ZURV)
to earn something by an action. *The children who work hard deserve to do well.*

dessert (dih-ZURT)
something sweet to eat after a meal.

diary (DIE-uh-ree)
a small notebook for writing daily happenings.

diary

different (DIF-ur-unt, DIF-runt)
not the same; unlike. *A pencil is different from a crayon.*

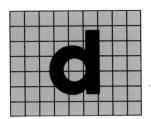

difficult (DIF-uh-KULT)
hard; not easy.

dig (dig)
to turn up or turn over soil.

dig

digital (DIJ-ih-tul)
giving information through numbers only. *My digital watch shows it's 12:34 P.M. exactly.*

dinner (DIN-ur)
the main meal of the day.

dinosaur (DIE-nuh-SOR)
a very large reptile that lived many millions of years ago.

dirty (DUR-tee)
needing to be washed or cleaned.

disappear (DIS-uh-PEER)
1. to go out of sight. *The magician seemed to disappear.*
2. to be or live no more. *What caused the dinosaurs to disappear millions of years ago?*

dinosaurs

disappoint (DIS-uh-POINT)
to make people unhappy by not doing what they had hoped.

dishonest (dis-ON-ist)
not able to be trusted; not telling the truth; crooked.

distance (DIS-tuns)
the space between two objects or places. *The distance between the towns is twenty miles, or thirty-two kilometers.*

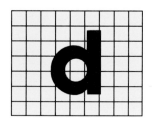

d

disturb (dih-STURB)
to upset or cause trouble.

ditch (dich)
a long, narrow trench dug in the ground to carry water.

dive (dive)
to jump headfirst downward, usually into water.

divide (dih-VIDE)
to separate something into smaller parts.

dog (dawg)
a four-legged, barking animal related to the wolf and
  often kept as a pet.

dog

doll (dahl)
a model of a real person used as a toy.

donkey (DONG-kee)
an animal that looks like a horse and has shaggy hair
  and long ears.

door (dohr)
a wooden or metal barrier that opens and closes on
  rooms, buildings, cars, and other things.

drag (drag)
to pull slowly and heavily.

dragon (DRAG-un)
in fairy tales, a winged, fire-breathing creature.

dragon

drain (drayn)
1. a pipe to carry waste water.
2. to carry waste water.

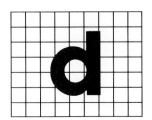

draw (draw)
to make a picture with a crayon, brush, pencil, or chalk.

dream (dreem)
the pictures and thoughts in the mind during sleep.

dress (dres)
1. clothing worn by ladies or girls.
2. to put on clothing.

drink (dringk)
to swallow a liquid.

drip (drip)
to fall in drops. *Water will drip from the leaky bucket.*

drive (drive)
1. to make a machine go.
2. a ride in a car. *We took a drive around the lake.*
3. to force along. *The dogs will drive the sheep over the hill.*

drop (drop)
1. a small amount of liquid in a round shape.
2. to let something fall.

drown (droun)
to die in water because of no air.

dry (dry)
without water; not wet.

duck (duk)
a swimming bird with a large, flat beak called a bill.

dust (dust)
tiny bits of dirt that can float in the air.

dress

duck

41

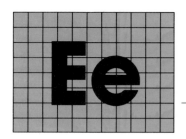

Ee

eagle (EE-gul)
a large bird with a sharp, curved beak and claws. *The eagle flew down and caught the rabbit hopping across the field.*

ear (eer)
1. the part of the body used for hearing.
2. the place on corn where the seeds grow.

early (UR-lee)
near the beginning or before the time agreed to.

earn (urn)
to get something in return for doing something; to deserve. *How much money did you earn working at the store?*

earth (urth)
1. the world where we live.
2. the ground or soil where we plant things.

earthquake (URTH-kwake)
a shaking of the surface of the earth.

east (eest)
one of the four main compass points; the opposite of west.

easy (EE-zee)
simple; not hard to do or understand.

eat (eet)
to bite food and then chew and swallow it.

edge (ej)
1. the cutting part of a knife or sword.
2. the end or rim of something. *The book fell over the edge of the table.*

eagle

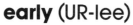

east

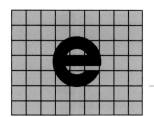

egg (eg)
something round, often with a shell, that is laid by female birds or other animals.

egg

electricity (ih-lek-TRIS-ih-tee, EE-lek-TRIS-ih-tee)
power used to make light and heat or drive machines.

elephant (EL-uh-funt)
a big animal with tusks and a long nose called a trunk.

elevator (EL-uh-VAY-tur)
a metal box or cage for people to ride in from one floor of a building to another.

elk (elk)
a large deer found in northern regions.

elephant

emergency (ih-MUR-jun-see)
a sudden or unexpected happening that calls for quick action.

empty (EMP-tee)
1. to take everything out of something.
2. with nothing in it.

end (end)
the last part of something. *She stayed until the end of the movie.*

enemy (EN-uh-mee)
a person or other creature that hates or fights against another.

energy (EN-ur-jee)
1. the strength to do things.
2. any form of power.

engine (EN-jun)
a machine that makes power to do work. *A car has an engine to make it go.*

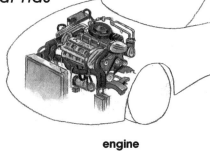

engine

enjoy (en-JOY)
to like doing something.
I enjoy eating ice cream.

enormous (ih-NOR-mus)
very, very large. *The Pacific Ocean is enormous.*

enough (ih-NUF)
just what is needed and no more.

entertain (EN-tur-TAIN)
to amuse and make people happy.

entrance (EN-truns)
the way in. *The entrance to the barn is over there.*

entrance (en-TRANS)
to fill with joy. *The cartoon movie will entrance you.*

envelope

envelope (EN-vuh-LOHP)
a folded cover for a letter.

equal (EE-kwul)
the same as.

equipment (ih-KWIP-munt)
the things needed to do something.

escape (ih-SKAPE)
to get away or get free.

evening (EEV-ning)
the time of day between sunset and dark.

exactly (eks-AKT-lee)
just right. *The two jigsaw pieces fitted exactly.*

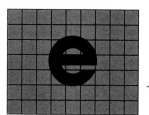

examination (eg-ZAM-uh-NAY-shun)
1. a test.
2. a careful look or search. *The doctor gave the sick boy an examination to find out why he was ill.*

excellent (EK-suh-lunt)
very, very good.

exchange (eks-CHAINJ)
to give one thing and get another back.

excite (ek-SITE)
to thrill or stir up strong feelings.

excuse (ek-SKYOOS; rhymes with "loose")
a reason for not doing something.

excuse (ek-SKYOOZ; rhymes with "lose")
to stop feeling angry at someone; to forgive.

exercise (EKS-ur-SIZE)
1. the training of mind or body.
2. a task to give practice.

exit (EG-zit, EK-sit)
the way out.

exit

expect (ek-SPEKT)
to think something will happen.

explain (ek-SPLAIN)
to make the meaning clear.

explode (ek-SPLOHD)
to blow up or burst with a loud bang.

eye (eye)
the part of the body used for seeing.

eye

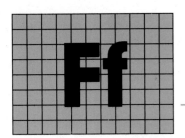

Ff

fabric (FAB-rik)
cloth or any material like cloth.

face (fays)
1. the front part of the head that includes the mouth, nose, and eyes.
2. the front of something, such as a clock.

face

fact (fakt)
something known to be true. *It is a fact that Davy Crockett died at the Alamo.*

factory (FAK-tuh-ree)
a building where things are made, usually with the help of machines.

fail (fail)
to try to do something but be unable to do it.

fall (fawl)
1. to drop or come down.
2. the season of the year between summer and winter.

false (fawls)
1. wrong; not true.
2. imitating the real thing. *Ann's mother has false teeth.*

family (FAM-uh-lee, FAM-lee)
people related to each other by birth or marriage, such as a father, mother, and their children.

family

famous (FAY-mus)
well known or widely talked about.

fan (fan)
1. a machine that makes a breeze.
2. one who is very fond of a sport, a hobby, or a famous person.

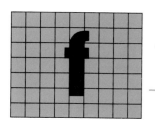

farm (farm)
land and buildings used for growing and storing food as well as keeping animals such as horses and cows.

farm

fast (fast)
1. very quick. *That horse is fast!*
2. to go without food. *Sick dogs will sometimes fast for more than a day.*

fasten (FAS-un)
to join together or lock.

fat (fat)
having a lot of flesh.

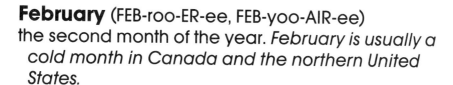

fasten

fault (fawlt)
anything that spoils or stops something from being perfect.

favorite (FAY-vur-it)
the person or thing liked best.

fear (feer)
a feeling of being in danger.

feather (FETH-ur)
one of the many pieces that make up the soft coat of a bird.

feather

February (FEB-roo-ER-ee, FEB-yoo-AIR-ee)
the second month of the year. *February is usually a cold month in Canada and the northern United States.*

feed (feed)
to give food to someone or something.

feel (feel)
to touch.

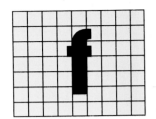

female (FEE-mail)
a girl or woman; usually any creature that can lay
 eggs or have babies.

fence (fens)
wooden posts or wire joined together and put around
 a piece of land.

fence

field (feeld)
1. an open, often flat piece of land.
2. a place where ball games are played.

fight (fite)
to go against someone or something; to try to beat.

fill (fil)
to leave no space for anything more.

film (film)
1. a roll of thin, flat material used for taking
 photographs in a camera.
2. a movie or motion picture.

find (find)
to see something that has been lost.

fine (fine)
1. of the best quality. *We ate dinner on the fine china.*
2. able to be enjoyed. *They had a fine time at
 the beach.*

finger (FING-gur)
one of five parts at the end of a hand.

finger

finish (FIN-ish)
1. to end. *Roy couldn't finish the last test question.*
2. the end of a race.

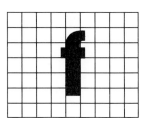

fire (fire)
1. to shoot a gun.
2. something burning.

fish (fish)
a cold-blooded animal that swims and can breathe
  underwater.

fish

fist (fist)
the hand with the fingers bent and pressed tightly
  together.

fit (fit)
1. in good health. *Playing sports will keep you fit.*
2. to be just the right size and shape. *My new shoes fit.*

fix (fiks)
1. to repair or mend something.
2. to hold steadily. *Fix your eyes on me.*

flag (flag)
a piece of cloth with a special pattern. *Each country
  has its own flag.*

flap (flap)
1. something hanging down loosely.
2. to move up and down. *Most birds flap their wings.*

flag

flat (flat)
smooth and level.

flavor (FLAY-vur)
the special taste of something eaten or drunk. *A
  lemon's flavor is sharp and sour.*

flesh (flesh)
the soft parts of the body covering the bones.

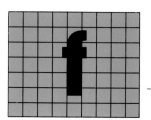

float (floht)
to rest on air or on the surface of water.

flood (flud)
a great amount of water from rain, rivers, or lakes
  flowing over roads, fields, and even houses.

floor (flor)
the part of a room for walking on.

flour (flour)
the powdery material made by grinding seeds of
  plants such as corn and wheat.

flour

flow (floh)
to move steadily.

flower (FLOU-ur)
the brightly colored part of a plant where the
  seeds are.

fly (fly)
1. to move through the air. *Most birds can fly.*
2. a small, winged insect.

fog (fog)
very thick mist near the ground.

fold (fold)
to bend or double something over.

fold

follow (FOL-oh)
to go or come after. *"Follow me," said the scout
  leader.*

food (food)
what is eaten to keep alive.

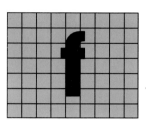

foot (foot)
1. a part of the body at the end of the leg used for standing and walking.
2. a length of twelve inches, or thirty and a half centimeters.

football (FOOT-bawl)
a game played on a large field by two teams of eleven players each; a ball is carried or thrown to each end of the field.

force (fors)
1. to make someone do something.
2. a group of people trained to work together.

forest (FOR-ist)
a large group of trees.

forest

forget (for-GET)
to let an idea go out of the mind; to fail to remember.

forgive (for-GIV)
to stop feeling angry at someone; to excuse.
Please forgive me for losing your purse.

fork (fork)
a tool with several long points used for eating or digging.

fox (foks)
a wild animal with a long, bushy tail and pointed ears and face that is smaller than a coyote.

fox

free (free)
1. not costing anything.
2. able to do as you like; not a prisoner.

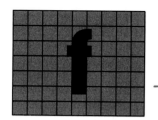

freeze (freez)
to turn into ice. *Water will freeze when it is very cold.*

fresh (fresh)
1. new; just made.
2. pure; clean. *That water is fresh.*

Friday (FRY-dee, FRY-day)
the sixth day of the week.

friend (frend)
a person you know and like very much.

frighten (FRITE-un)
to make someone afraid.

frog (frog)
a small amphibian with webbed feet that lives in or
near water and hops.

front (frunt)
the part that faces forward; the most forward part.

fruit (froot)
the part of a plant or tree that holds the seeds and
can often be eaten.

fuel (FYOO-ul)
anything burned to make heat or to give energy.

full (ful)
holding so much that there is no room for more.

funny (FUN-ee)
making one laugh. *Jokes are funny.*

fur (fur)
the soft coat of hair covering an animal's body.

freeze

frogs

fur

gallon (GAL-un)
a volume equal to 4 quarts, or 3.8 liters.

game (gaym)
1. something played that uses a set of rules.
2. wild animals hunted for sport.

gap (gap)
a space or opening between two things.

garage (guh-RAHZH, guh-RAHJ)
a place where cars are kept.

garage

garden (GAR-dun)
a piece of ground for growing flowers, fruit, or
  vegetables.

gas (gas)
1. something like air, not solid and not liquid. *We use
  gas for heating and cooking.*
2. the liquid fuel put into cars to make them go.

gate (gate)
a wooden or metal barrier that can be moved to open
  or close an opening in a wall or fence.

gate

generous (JEN-ur-us)
ready to give things to people who need or want
  them.

gentle (JEN-tul)
not rough.

ghost (gohst)
what some people say is the spirit of a dead person
  that does not leave the world.

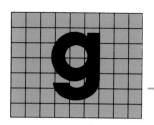

g

giant (JI-unt)
1. a large person or thing.
2. huge.

giraffe (ju-RAF)
an animal from Africa, with spotted skin, a long
neck, and long legs.

give (giv)
to hand over something.

glass (glas)
1. a hard material you can usually see through.
2. a container made for drinking.

glass

glasses (GLAS-iz)
lenses held together in a frame to help a person see
better; also called eyeglasses.

glider (GLY-dur)
a light airplane with no engine.

glue (gloo)
something used to stick things together.

gnaw (naw)
to chew and bite with the front teeth. *The rabbit began
to gnaw a carrot.*

goal (gohl)
something to work and hope for. *My goal is to get
good grades in school.*

goat (goht)
an animal that has pointed horns and
a beard and is about as big as a sheep.

goat

goggles (GOG-ulz)
a large pair of glasses meant to protect the eyes.

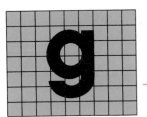

gold (gohld)
a valuable yellow metal.

golf (golf)
a game played with a small, hard ball and a set of sticks called clubs.

good (good)
1. well-behaved.
2. of high quality. *Joan's good work won a prize.*

gorilla (gu-RIL-uh)
the largest kind of ape; it is black or gray and lives in the forests of Africa.

gorilla

government (GUV-urn-munt, GUV-ur-munt)
the group of people who run a country.

grade (grayd)
1. to mark a test or paper for good ideas.
2. the mark showing how well you did in school or on a test or paper.

gradual (GRAJ-oo-ul)
happening slowly.

grain (grayn)
1. the seeds of plants such as wheat and oats.
2. a very small piece of something. *It is difficult to see one grain of salt.*
3. the lines in wood.

gram (gram)
a weight equal to $1/1{,}000$ kilogram, or 0.035 ounce.

grape (grayp)
a small, round fruit that grows in bunches on a vine.

grape

55

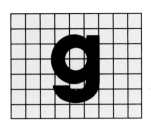

grass (gras)
a plant with thin, green leaves grown in fields and
   for lawns.

grass

gravity (GRAV-ih-tee)
the pull of the earth that makes things fall down when
   thrown up in the air or dropped.

great (grayt)
1. large.
2. very important. *George Washington was a great
   leader.*

greedy (GREE-dee)
wanting more than what is needed; wanting too much.

ground (ground)
1. the earth that we walk on.
2. crushed into small pieces. *Coffee beans are ground
   to make coffee.*

group (groop)
a number of people or things all together.

grow (groh)
to get bigger.

guard (gard)
1. to look after or keep something or someone safe.
2. a person who keeps something or someone safe.

guess (ges)
to say or think something without real knowledge or
   strong reason.

gun (gun)
a weapon for shooting bullets or other things.

gun

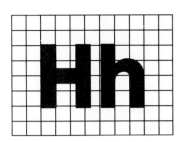

habit (HAB-it)
a thing done so often that it is done almost without thinking. *Brushing your teeth is a good habit.*

hail (hayl)
frozen rain that falls as small, hard pieces.

hair (hayr)
the thin, soft growth on the heads and bodies of mammals.

hamburger (HAM-bur-gur)
1. ground meat.
2. a sandwich made of cooked ground meat inside a sliced roll or bun.

hamburger

hammer (HAM-ur)
a tool with a wooden or metal handle and usually a heavy metal head that is used for hitting things such as nails.

hand (hand)
the part of the body at the end of the arm.

handle (HAN-dul)
1. the part of something held in the hand that helps you hold or carry it.
2. to touch something with the hands.

hand

hang (hang)
1. to fasten something to a wall or ceiling high enough so that it does not touch the ground.
2. to bend down. *The snow on the branches made them hang lower than usual.*

happen (HAP-un)
to take place. *Accidents can happen to anyone.*

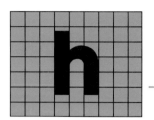

happy (HAP-ee)
full of joy.

harbor (HAR-bur)
a place where ships are safe from storms.

hard (hard)
1. firm and solid like a rock.
2. not easy to do.

hat (hat)
a covering worn on the head.

hat

hate (hayt)
to have a very strong feeling against.

head (hed)
1. the part of the body above the neck.
2. the person in charge of something. *She was the head of our school trip.*

healthy (HEL-thee)
free from illness.

hear (heer)
to take in sounds through the ears; to be aware of sounds. *If you listen carefully, you can hear the water dripping.*

helicopter

heavy (HEV-ee)
of great weight. *My bed is heavy.*

helicopter (HEL-uh-KOP-tur)
a flying machine without wings that is lifted into the air by blades turning around and around.

helmet (HEL-mit)
a hard kind of hat worn to protect the head.

helmet

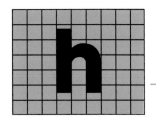

help (help)
to make things easier for someone by
  sharing the work. *The children can help by washing
  the dishes.*

hide (hide)
1. to put or keep out of sight.
2. the outer covering of an animal; skin.

high (hi)
a long way above the ground.

hill (hil)
a place where the ground is higher than the land
  around it, but not as high as a mountain.

hills

hips (hips)
the place on the body below the waist where
  a person's legs start.

hit (hit)
1. to strike something.
2. a very popular song or record.

hobby (HOB-ee)
something people like to do for fun.

hockey (HOK-ee)
a team game played on ice, with a puck and a stick
  that is curved at the end.

hold (hohld)
1. to have something in the hand.
2. the part of a ship where a lot of heavy things
  are kept.

hockey

hole (hohl)
an opening. *The rabbit ran into a hole in the ground.*

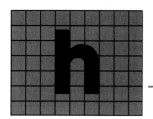

holiday (HOL-ih-DAY)
a day when there is no work or school.

hollow (HOL-oh)
having a hole on the inside. *The squirrel hid inside the hollow tree.*

home (hohm)
a place where a person lives.

honest (AHN-ist)
able to be trusted; truthful; not lying or stealing. *The used car salesman was an honest man.*

honey (HUN-ee)
a sweet, sticky food that bees make from the liquid they collect from flowers.

honey

hoof (hoof)
the hard covering on the toes of animals such as deer, cattle, and sheep.

hook (hook)
a bent piece of metal that is used to catch fish or to hang things.

hop (hop)
to jump.

hope (hohp)
to wish for something to happen or come true.

horn (horn)
1. hard bone growing out of the head of some animals.
2. a musical instrument. *Louis Armstrong could really play the horn.*

horses

horse (hors)
an animal used for riding or pulling vehicles.

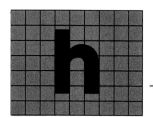

hospital (HOS-pih-tul)
a building where sick or hurt people are taken care of.

hot (hot)
very, very warm.

hour (our)
sixty minutes.

house (hous)
a building where people live.

house

hug (hug)
to put your arms around someone or something and
  hold on.

huge (hyooj)
very, very big. *The Empire State Building in New York
  City is huge.*

hungry (HUNG-gree)
needing or wanting food.

hunt (hunt)
1. to try to catch wild animals for food.
2. to look carefully for something.
3. a chase.

hurricane (HUR-uh-KAIN)
a very bad storm with strong winds that starts on the
  ocean and can move over land near the ocean.

hurry (HUR-ee)
to move very quickly.

hurry

hurt (hurt)
to make someone feel pain.

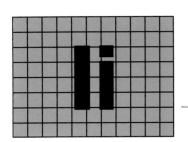

ice (ice)
frozen water.

icicle (EYE-si-kul)
a hanging piece of ice.

idea (eye-DEE-uh)
a thought in the head.

ill (il)
not well; sick.

imaginary (ih-MAJ-uh-NER-ee)
made up in your mind; not real.

imitate (IM-ih-TAIT)
to try to do exactly the same as somebody else;
  to copy.

important (im-POHR-tunt)
1. serious; meaning a great deal. *It is important to
   John to finish first in the race.*
2. having power or control. *The mayor is an important
   person in this town.*

impossible (im-POS-uh-bul)
not able to be done.

inch (inch)
one twelfth of a foot, or 2.54 centimeters.

information (IN-fur-MAY-shun)
ideas and facts that are known or believed to be true.

injure (IN-jur)
to hurt someone or something.

ink (ingk)
a colored liquid used for writing or printing.

ice

ink

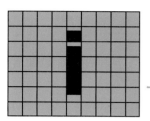

insect (IN-sekt)
a small animal with six legs.

instrument (IN-struh-ment)
1. a tool making a job easier.
2. something on which music is played. *The instrument Claire likes to play is the piano.*

intense (in-TENS)
very great or strong.

insect

interesting (IN-tuh-RES-ting, IN-trih-sting)
holding your attention; making you want to know more.

interrupt (IN-tuh-RUPT)
to speak when someone else is speaking; to butt in.

invent (in-VENT)
to think up or make something new.

invisible (in-VIZ-uh-bul)
not able to be seen.

invite (in-VITE)
to ask someone to do something or go somewhere.

iron (EYE-urn)
1. a strong, hard metal.
2. a tool, when heated, that is used for smoothing clothes or cloth.
3. to smooth clothes or cloth.

island (EYE-lund)
a piece of land with water all around it.

island

itch (ich)
a feeling on the skin that makes you want to scratch it.

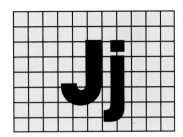

Jj

jab (jab)
to push quickly with something sharp. *Cathy began to jab the leather with her needle.*

jagged (JAG-id)
having rough, sharp points.

jail (jail)
a place where people who break the law have to go when they are caught.

January (JAN-yoo-ER-ee)
the first month of the year; it has thirty-one days.

jar (jar)
a container made of pottery or glass with a very wide opening at the top.

jeans (jeenz)
pants made usually of a tough cotton cloth called denim.

jelly (JEL-ee)
a sweet food made by boiling fruit and sugar together until a thick liquid is formed.

jewel (JOO-ul)
a valuable stone, such as a diamond.

jewelry

jewelry (JOO-ul-ree)
something to wear that is often made of jewels and gold or silver.

jigsaw puzzle (JIG-saw)
a puzzle picture made by fitting the pieces together.

jigsaw puzzle

job (job)
work; what people do to earn money.

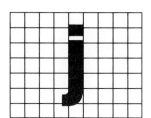

jog (johg)
to run at a slow, steady speed.

join (join)
1. to fasten together. *We can all join hands to make a circle.*
2. to become a member of a group, such as a choir or a club. *When I am old enough, I am going to join the Marine Corps.*

joint (joint)
the point where two things are held together.

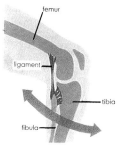
joint

joke (johk)
something said or written to make people laugh.

journey (JUR-nee)
to travel from one place to another.

jug (jug)
a container with a handle, used for pouring liquids.

juice (joos)
the liquid in fruit, meat, and vegetables.

July (Joo-LIE; Juh-LIE)
the seventh month of the year; it has thirty-one days.

jump (jump)
to leap into the air with all feet off the ground.

June (Joon)
the sixth month of the year; it has thirty days.

jump

jungle (JUNG-gul)
land in hot, wet climates where many bushes, trees, and other plants grow in thick groups.

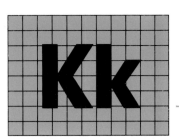

Kk

kangaroo (KANG-guh-ROO)
an Australian animal with strong back legs for jumping and a skin pouch on its body for carrying babies.

kangaroo

keep (keep)
to hold on to something for yourself.

kettle (KET-ul)
a metal container with a handle on top that is mostly used for boiling water.

key (kee)
1. a piece of metal used for locking and unlocking.
2. one of the parts pressed on a typewriter or piano to make it work.

kick (kik)
to hit with the foot. *Ernie could kick a football very far.*

kill (kil)
to take life away by force.

kilogram (KIL-uh-GRAM)
a weight equal to 1,000 grams, or 2.2 pounds.

kilometer (KIL-uh-MEE-tur, kih-LOM-ih-tur)
a length equal to 1,000 meters, or 0.62 mile.

kind (kind)
1. friendly and helpful.
2. a group of people, other animals, or things that are like one another in some way.

king (king)
a male ruler of a country, who often gets his job because he belongs to the ruling family.

king

kiss (kis)
to touch someone with the lips.

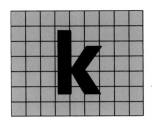

kit (kit)
a set of things needed for making something, such as a model airplane.

kitchen (KICH-un)
the room where food is prepared and cooked for eating. *Robin made cookies in the kitchen.*

kitchen

kite (kite)
1. a toy made of paper or cloth on a wooden frame and flown on the end of a long string.
2. a large bird that kills animals for food.

knack (nak)
special skill or ability for doing something easily. *She has a knack for fixing things.*

knife (nife)
a cutting tool; a flat piece of metal with a sharp edge and a handle.

knit (nit)
to join threads tightly together by using needles.

knit

knock (nok)
1. to hit something hard.
2. to push or hit something and make it fall.
3. to make a pounding noise. *The car engine started to knock.*

knot (not)
1. the place where string or rope is tied.
2. a measure of speed; one sea mile (1.852 kilometers) per hour.
3. a round, very hard place in a piece of wood.

know (noh)
to be sure about something; to understand.

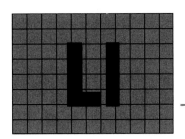

Ll

label (LAY-bul)
something fastened or pasted on an object that describes what it is or what is inside.

label

laboratory (LAB-ruh-TOR-ee, lab-OR-uh-TOR-ee)
a room or building where students or scientists study and test things.

laces (LAYS-uz)
pieces of cloth or string used to fasten things such as shoes.

ladder (LAD-ur)
steps with wooden or metal bars attached between two long pieces of wood or metal.

lake (layk)
a large body of water surrounded by land.

land (land)
1. ground that is not covered by water.
2. to come to the ground from the air or water.

language (LANG-gwij)
the words used by people when they speak or write.

lasso

large (larj)
very big.

lasso (LAS-oh, la-SOO)
a long rope with a sliding loop at one end, used to capture cattle and wild horses.

late (layt)
coming after a time agreed to; not early.

laugh (laf)
the noise people make when they are happy or think something is very funny.

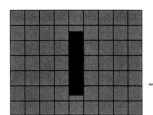

laundromat (LON-druh-MAT)
a place where people put money in machines that
  wash and dry clothes.

law (law)
a rule the government makes.

layer (LAY-ur)
a single, flat piece or thickness lying on top of
  or beneath something else.

layer

lazy (LAY-zee)
not wanting to work.

lead (leed; rhymes with "feed")
to go first and show the way.

lead (led; rhymes with "bed")
1. a heavy, gray metal.
2. the part of a pencil used for writing.

leaf (leef)
one of the thin, flat, green parts of a plant.

leaf

leak (leek)
1. a hole or crack that lets gas or liquid escape.
2. to enter or escape through an opening.

learn (lurn)
to find out about things or how to do something.

leather (LETH-ur)
material made from animal skin that has been
  cleaned, with all hair removed.

leave (leev)
1. to go away from.
2. to let something stay where it is.

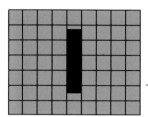

left (left)
the opposite side of right.

leg (leg)
a long part of the lower body that is used for walking.

lend (lend)
to let someone have or use something for a short time.

length (lenth)
how long something is.

lens (lenz)
a curved piece of glass used in such things as
eyeglasses and cameras.

letter (LET-ur)
1. a piece of writing put in an envelope to send
to someone.
2. one of the parts of an alphabet.

letter

level (LEV-ul)
flat and even. *Tennis is played on a level surface.*

lever (LEV-ur, LEE-vur)
1. a strong bar used to lift or move things. *Jimmy used
a lever to push the huge rock from the road.*
2. a small bar or rod on a machine. *When the man
pulled the lever, all the lights went on.*

library (LIE-brer-ee)
1. a collection of books.
2. a place where books are kept.

lick (lik)
to touch something with the tongue.

lick

lid (lid)
a container top that can be taken off.

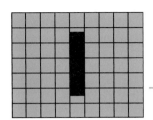

lie (lie)
1. something untrue, either said or written.
2. to rest in a flat position.

life (life)
1. the time between birth and death.
2. being alive; being able to breathe, eat, sleep, and move.

light (lite)
1. something that shines brightly.
2. not heavy; easy to lift.
3. to set on fire.

lightning (LITE-ning)
a very bright flash of light seen in the sky during a very bad storm.

like (like)
1. almost the same as something else. *A frog is like a toad.*
2. to enjoy. *Most children like to play games.*

limb (lim)
1. a leg or an arm.
2. the branch of a tree.

line (line)
1. a long, thin mark.
2. a row formed by things or people. *The children stood in line beside the bus.*

lion (LIE-un)
a large, wild animal of the cat family.

liquid (LIK-wid)
something that can be poured; not a solid or a gas.

lightning

lion

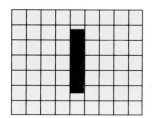

list (list)
1. things written down in a series, usually one under another. *Please make a list of names.*
2. to write things down in a series.

listen (LIS-un)
to try to hear sounds with the ears.

liter (LEE-tur)
a volume equal to 1.06 liquid quarts.

live (liv; rhymes with "give")
to be or stay alive. *Did anyone live through the plane crash?*

live (live; rhymes with "dive")
having life; alive. *There are no live dinosaurs anywhere in the world.*

lizard (LIZ-urd)
a reptile with four short legs and a tail.

lizard

load (lohd)
1. something carried. *In the truck was a load of potatoes.*
2. to prepare a gun for firing.

lock (lok)
1. something needing a key to open it. *The door has a lock.*
2. to fasten something using a key. *Jerome locked the car before we went into the supermarket.*

locomotive (LOH-kuh-MOH-tiv)
an engine used to pull cars along railroad tracks.

locomotive

lodge (loj)
a small house or shelter.

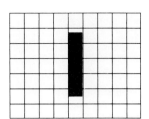

log (log)
1. a long, thick piece of a tree used for building or burning.
2. a record of things that have happened.

lonely (LOHN-lee)
feeling sad, alone, or without friends.

long (long)
1. far from one end to the other. *It is a long way from Maine to Hawaii.*
2. to want something badly. *They long for a vacation.*

look (look)
to use your eyes to see something.

loose (loos)
not fastened properly; free to move.

lose (looz)
1. to put something in a place and then not be able to find it.
2. to be beaten in a game.

loud (loud)
very noisy; easily heard.

love (luv)
1. to like someone very, very much.
2. the feeling of liking someone very much.

luck (luk)
something good or bad that happens without people's control.

lump (lump)
1. a small piece of something, such as clay or coal.
2. a swelling or bump.

logs

loose

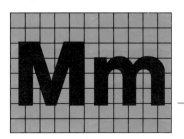

Mm

machine (muh-SHEEN)
a thing used to help people work more easily. *With this electric sewing machine, I can make my own clothes.*

magazine (MAG-uh-ZEEN)
a thin book that is usually printed once a week or once a month.

magazine

magic (MAJ-ik)
1. happenings that are hard to explain and seem to be beyond ordinary human power.
2. a way to entertain people by clever tricks.

magnet (MAG-nit)
a piece of iron or steel with the power to pull other pieces of iron or steel toward it.

magnet

mail (mayl)
letters or packages sent to people.

main (main)
1. most important.
2. a pipe that carries gas, water, or electricity to buildings.

male (mayl)
a boy or a man; animals that can become fathers.

mammal (MAM-ul)
a warm-blooded animal that can control its own body temperature. *A female mammal feeds milk to its young.*

map (map)
a drawing of a place or country as it looks from the sky. *A map helps people find their way.*

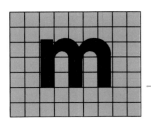

march (march)
to walk in measured steps at a steady rate.

March (March)
the third month of the year; it has thirty-one days.

mark (mark)
1. a sign showing something.
2. a spot or stain.
3. to show by a sign. *The pirate put an "X" on the map to mark where the gold was buried.*

marry (MAR-ee)
to become husband and wife.

material (muh-TEER-ee-ul)
any stuff used for making things. *Wool is just one material from which clothes are made.*

may (may)
to be allowed to. *May I go to the party?*

May (May)
the fifth month of the year; it has thirty-one days.

meal (meel)
breakfast, lunch, dinner, or supper.

measure (MEZH-ur)
to find out the size, amount, length, or weight of anything.

meat (meet)
the flesh of animals used for food.

medicine (MED-ih-sin)
a pill or drink swallowed by a sick person to improve his or her health.

march

meat

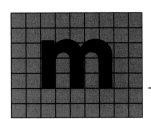

meet (meet)
to come together. *Maria told George to meet her at the theater.*

melt (melt)
to change a solid into a liquid by using heat. *If you leave ice cubes out in the sun, they will melt.*

melt

member (MEM-bur)
one of the people, animals, or things belonging to a group.

mend (mend)
to fix or repair; to put right again. *I had to mend a hole in my sock.*

message (MES-ij)
words sent from one person to another.

metal (MET-ul)
a hard material such as iron, steel, gold, copper, or silver.

meter (MEE-tur)
1. an instrument for measuring. *A gas meter measures how much gas is burned.*
2. a length of 3.28 feet.

middle (MID-ul)
halfway; a place that is the same distance from each end or side.

midnight (MID-nite)
twelve o'clock at night.

mile (mile)
a length of 5,280 feet, or 1,610 meters.

midnight

milk (milk)
the white liquid made by female mammals to
 feed their young. *We usually drink cow's milk.*

milk

millimeter (MIL-ih-MEE-tur)
a length of $1/1{,}000$ meter, or 0.0394 inch.

mind (mind)
what a person thinks, learns, knows, remembers, and
 understands with; brain.

mineral (MIN-ur-ul, MIN-rul)
a material that makes up rocks and other nonliving
 parts of the earth.

mint (mint)
1. a place where coins are made.
2. a small, green plant with a strong taste.
3. a candy flavored with mint.

minute (MIN-it)
sixty seconds.

mirror (MIR-ur)
a special piece of glass that you can see yourself in.

mirror

miserable (MIS-ur-uh-bul, MIZ-ruh-bul)
very unhappy.

miss (mis)
1. a polite title for a girl or woman who is not married.
2. to fail to hit.
3. to notice when someone or something is not there.

mist (mist)
a thin fog.

mistake (mi-STAYK)
something done wrongly; an error.

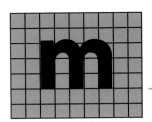

mister (MIS-tur)
a polite title for a man.

mix (miks)
to stir different things together.

mixture (MIKS-chur)
something that is made by mixing two or more things.

model (MOD-ul)
1. a small but very good copy of something.
2. a man or woman who shows off clothes.

Monday (MUN-dee, MUN-day)
the second day of the week.

money (MUN-ee)
coins or bills used to buy things.

money

monkey (MUNG-kee)
a small, furry animal that has a long tail and is good at
  climbing trees.

month (munth)
one of twelve parts in a year.

moon (moon)
a large, round object that moves around a planet. *The
  moon circles the earth.*

moose (moos)
a large animal with flat antlers that is related to
  the deer.

moose

morning (MOR-ning)
the part of the day between midnight and noon.

mound (mound)
a hill or pile of earth, stones, or other solid material.

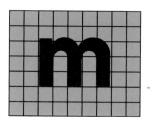

mountain (MOUN-tun)
land much higher than a hill.

mouse (mous)
a small animal with a pointed nose and a long, thin tail.

mouse

mouth (mouth)
1. the opening in the face for taking in food and drink, and for talking.
2. the place where a river meets another river or the ocean.

move (moov)
1. to put something in another place.
2. to put something into action.
3. to get from one place to another.

movie (MOO-vee)
a motion picture, or film, seen in a theater.

mud (mud)
a soft and sticky mixture of earth and water.

muscle (MUS-ul)
a part of the body joined to a bone that loosens and tightens to help the body move.

museum (myoo-ZEE-um)
a building where interesting things are put on show for people to look at.

mushroom (MUSH-room)
a small, white and brown plant shaped like an umbrella; some types can be eaten.

mushroom

music (MYOO-zik)
1. pleasing sounds made by instruments or singing.
2. the symbols on paper that people read to make tunes.

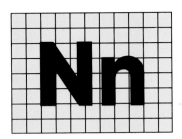

Nn

nail (nail)
1. a thin, pointed piece of metal often used to join two pieces of wood.
2. the hard piece at the end of a finger or a toe.

nail

name (naym)
what someone or something is called.

narrow (NAR-roh)
not wide. *A sidewalk is too narrow for a truck.*

nasty (NAS-tee)
mean; unkind; painful; hurtful.

nation (NAY-shun)
a country; all the people who live in a country.

nature (NAY-chur)
all plants, animals, and anything not made by people.

navy (NAY-vee)
the warships and sailors of a country.

near (neer)
close. *I was so near the bird that I could touch it.*

neat (neet)
clean and in order.

needle (NEED-ul)
a long, pointed tool with a hole in one end that is used for sewing.

neighbor (NAY-bur)
a person who lives near you.

nest (nest)
a home an animal makes for its babies.

nest

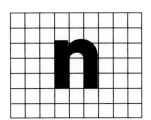

n

net (net)
pieces of thread or rope tied together to make a trap or holder.

new (noo, nyoo)
fresh; just made; not known before.

nice (nice)
kind; friendly; helpful. *It was very nice of Joan to work on the project with us.*

night (nite)
the time between evening and morning when the sky is dark.

noise (noiz)
a sound, often loud or not enjoyable.

noon (noon)
the middle of the day; twelve o'clock.

north (north)
one of the four main compass points; the opposite of south.

nose (nohz)
the part of the face for breathing and smelling things.

November (Noh-VEM-bur)
the eleventh month of the year; it has thirty days.

number (NUM-bur)
a word or sign telling how many. *The number two (2) comes before the number three (3).*

nut (nut)
1. a fruit or seed with a hard shell.
2. the small block of metal that fits around a bolt, which is like a nail with metal threads cut into it.

net

nose

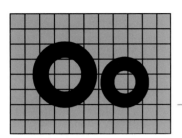

object (OB-jekt)
1. a thing that can be touched or seen. *Fred held a tiny object in his hand.*
2. a goal or purpose. *What is the object of this game?*

object (ob-JEKT)
to be against; to be unhappy with. *"I object to the nasty way you're behaving!" said the man angrily.*

ocean (OH-shun)
the salt water that covers about three quarters of the earth.

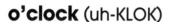

ocean

o'clock (uh-KLOK)
the time by the clock. *The party begins at four o'clock.*

October (Ok-TOH-bur)
the tenth month of the year; it has thirty-one days.

octopus (OK-tuh-pus)
a sea animal that has eight arms to grab hold of its prey.

octopus

odd (od)
1. not even; unable to be grouped in twos. *Three (3) is an odd number.*
2. strange.

offer (AW-fur)
1. to show or say that one is ready to do something. *Can we offer you help in moving that log?*
2. saying what you think something is worth. *His final offer was fifty dollars for the bicycle.*

officer (AW-fih-sur)
a person who gives orders in the army, navy, air force, police, or fire service.

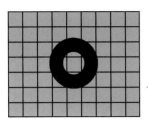

oil (oil)
a greasy liquid we take from animals or plants or out of the earth.

old (ohld)
living a long time; not young; not new.

open (OH-pun)
not shut; allowing things to pass in and out.

open

opposite (OP-uh-zit)
1. on the other side. *They lived in the house opposite us.*
2. as different as it possibly can be. *Up is the opposite of down.*

order (OR-dur)
1. to arrange neatly or in a good way.
2. to tell someone to do something.

ordinary (OR-duh-NER-ee)
common and everyday; not special.

orphan (OR-fun)
someone whose parents are dead.

ounce (ouns)
a weight equal to one sixteenth of a pound, or 28.35 grams.

oven

oven (UV-un)
a closed space where food is baked.

own (ohn)
to have something that belongs to you. *I own three baseballs and two bats.*

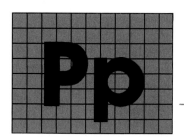

Pp

pack (pak)
1. to put things into a box, bag, or case.
2. a bag to be carried on the back.
3. a group of things that are all the same, like a pack of cards or a pack of animals.

package (PAK-ij)
a small box or container, often wrapped, that holds something.

paddle (PAD-ul)
a wooden or plastic tool with a long handle and a flat blade that is often used to push a canoe or boat through water.

paddle

page (payj)
one side of a sheet of paper in a book or magazine.

pain (payn)
the feeling one has after being injured.

paint (paynt)
1. a colored liquid put onto a wall, wood, paper, or canvas.
2. to cover something with paint.

painting (PAYN-ting)
a picture that has been made with paint.

pair (pair)
a set of two.

pair

pajamas (puh-JAH-muz, puh-JAM-uz)
a loose shirt and pants worn in bed.

pants (pants)
clothing worn from the waist to the feet, with a separate section for each leg.

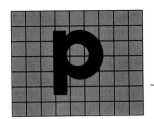

paper (PAY-pur)
material used for writing, printing, or drawing on.

parachute (PAHR-uh-SHOOT)
a large piece of cloth shaped like an umbrella that is
   used for floating safely down from a flying airplane.

parachute

park (park)
1. an open space in a town or city that is set aside for
   people to enjoy themselves.
2. to leave a car in a particular place.

part (part)
1. a piece.
2. to split something; to separate. *I like to part my hair
   down the middle.*

particular (par-TIK-yuh-lur)
just that person or thing and not others of the same
   kind.

party (PAR-tee)
a group of people having fun together.

pass (pas)
1. to go by; to get ahead of.
2. to get a special number of answers right on a test.
3. to hand something to someone.
4. a narrow opening between two mountains.
5. a ticket that lets a person in for nothing.

paste (payst)
a thick mixture used for sticking things together.

patient (PAY-shunt)
1. able to wait calmly for a long time.
2. a person who is being helped by a doctor, dentist,
   or nurse.

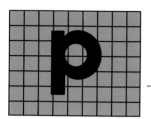

pattern (PAT-urn)
1. a plan or model to follow or copy when making something.
2. a drawing used over and over again to decorate something.
3. a set of things done over and over again.

paw (paw)
the foot of an animal with claws.

pay (pay)
to give money for work done or for something bought.

peach (peech)
a juicy fruit with a soft, orange-colored skin.

pear

pear (pair)
a juicy brown, yellow, or green fruit shaped like a cone and with a round bottom.

pedal (PED-ul)
the part of a machine worked by the foot, such as a bicycle pedal.

peel (peel)
1. the outer covering of a vegetable or a fruit.
2. to take off the outer covering. *Please peel an orange for me.*

pen (pen)
a tool that is used for writing with ink.

pencil (PEN-sul)
a tool for writing, often made of wood, with a thin strip of black or colored material in the middle.

pens

penguin (PEN-gwin, PENG-win)
a black and white swimming bird with webbed feet.

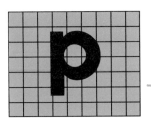

penny (PEN-ee)
a coin worth one cent.

perfect (PUR-fikt)
having nothing wrong with it.

period (PEER-ee-ud)
a particular length of time.

person (PUR-sun)
a human being; a man, woman, or child.

pet (pet)
an animal kept and taken care of at home. *My favorite pet is a dog.*

phone (fohn)
short word for telephone.

photograph (FOH-tuh-GRAF)
a picture taken with a camera.

photograph

pick (pik)
1. to choose. *The coach will pick his football team.*
2. to gather, like flowers or fruit. *The girls will pick some flowers for you.*
3. a tool with a curved blade fastened to a long handle that is used to break rock or hard ground.

picture (PIK-chur)
a drawn, painted, or photographed copy of something.

piece (peese)
a part of something, such as a piece of cake.

pig (pig)
a farm animal raised for its meat, called pork.

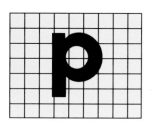

p

pillow (PIL-oh)
a cloth bag filled with soft material such as feathers.

pin (pin)
a thin stick of metal with a flat head at one end and a point at the other that is used to fasten things together.

pipe (pipe)
1. a hollow tube to carry gas or liquid from one place to another.
2. a tube ending in a small bowl that is used for smoking tobacco.

pirate (PIE-rut)
a robber who steals from ships at sea.

pitch (pich)
1. to throw, as a pitcher does in baseball.
2. to set up a tent.

pitch

place (plase)
a particular spot; the position where something is. *Put your jewelry in a safe place.*

plan (plan)
1. a drawing that shows what a thing looks like from above.
2. to think about how to do something.

planet (PLAN-it)
one of the huge objects, such as the earth, that goes around the sun.

planet

plant (plant)
1. anything that grows in soil.
2. to place something in the ground to grow.

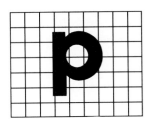

plastic (PLAS-tik)
a material made from oil and used to make many
  things, such as toys, buckets, and cups.

plate (playt)
a flat dish for putting food on.

platform (PLAT-form)
1. a raised floor in a hall; a stage.
2. the part in a railroad station where people wait for
  a train.

play (play)
1. a story that is acted out.
2. to enjoy oneself; to have fun. *"Let's play
  hide-and-seek."*
3. to make sounds on a musical instrument.

platform

poison (POY-zun)
something that causes illness or death when taken
  into the body.

pond (pond)
a small lake.

pond

poor (por)
1. having very little money.
2. badly done. *The repairs were so poor that the car
  still would not run.*

popular (POP-yuh-lur)
liked by a lot of people.

position (puh-ZISH-un)
1. the place where something is at a particular
  moment.
2. job. *Phyllis took a new position at the bank.*

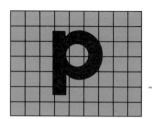

poster (POH-stur)
a large sign or picture.

pound (pound)
1. a weight of 16 ounces, or 450 grams.
2. to hit very hard again and again.

pour (por)
1. to make a liquid run out in a steady stream. *Will you pour me a glass of milk?*
2. to rain a lot.

pour

powder (POU-dur)
many tiny bits of something, often as fine as dust.

power (POU-ur)
1. strength.
2. energy, such as electricity, that can be used to make things work.
3. to be in control of other people.

prehistoric (PREE-hih-STOR-ik)
belonging to a time before history was written down.

present (PREZ-unt)
1. a gift.
2. the time right now.
3. here; not somewhere else.

present

president (PREZ-ih-dent)
the leader of a government, a business, or a club. *Carol was president of the school's science club.*

press (pres)
1. to push.
2. to smooth clothes or cloth; to iron.

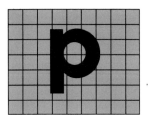

pretend (prih-TEND)
to make believe.

pretty (PRIT-ee)
nice to look at.

prey (pray)
an animal hunted and eaten by other animals.

price (prise)
the amount of money needed to buy something; the cost.

price

problem (PROB-lum)
something difficult or confusing.

program (PROH-gram, PROH-grum)
1. a list of things to be seen or heard at a concert or a play.
2. a list of instructions for a computer.
3. a show or other item on radio or television.

project (PROJ-ekt)
1. a study of something.
2. a large job that is done in several parts, such as building a dam.

protect (pruh-TEKT)
to keep people or things from harm or damage.

pull (pul)
to drag something.

pull

push (push)
to move something by putting force against it. *Please push the door open.*

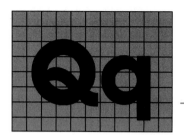

Qq

quality (KWOL-ih-tee)
how good or bad something is when compared to other things.

quantity (KWON-tih-tee)
the number or size of something. *Dad ordered a large quantity of sand for the sandbox.*

quarrel (KWAR-ul, KWOR-ul)
to talk angrily with someone who does not agree.

quart (kwort)
a volume equal to ¼ gallon, or 0.95 liter.

queen (kween)
a woman ruler of a country, who often gets her job because she belongs to the ruling family.

queen

question (KWES-chun)
a sentence asking something. *"What is the capital of Spain?" was a test question.*

quick (kwik)
very fast; lively.

quiet (KWY-it)
making no noise; still.

quit (kwit)
1. to stop doing something.
2. to stop trying or to give up.

quiz (kwiz)
a short test.

quote (kwoht)
to say or write exactly what someone else has said or written.

quiz

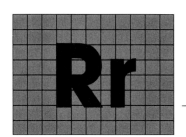

rabbit (RAB-it)
a small, quick animal with soft fur and long ears that
  hops.

rabbit

race (rase)
1. a contest where a person tries to do something
  better or faster than the others.
2. to try to beat someone in a competition, usually for
  speed.

radar (RAY-dar)
a way of guiding ships and airplanes, especially in fog
  or at night, through the use of radio waves.

radio (RAY-dee-OH)
an instrument for sending and receiving sounds
  by electric signals through the air.

radar

rail (rayl)
a bar of metal or wood used to hold something up or
  back. *The rail was along the edge of the cliff.*

railroad (RAIL-rohd)
the track of rails on which trains run.

rain (rayn)
drops of water that fall from clouds.

rainbow (RAYN-boh)
the arch of seven colors seen in the sky when the sun
  shines through rain or mist. *The colors of the rainbow
  are red, orange, yellow, green, blue, indigo, and
  violet.*

ranch (ranch)
a piece of land where cattle, horses, or sheep
  are raised.

rainbow

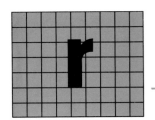

rat (rat)
a long-tailed animal with sharp teeth; it looks like a
  large mouse.

rat

raw (raw)
uncooked. *Some Japanese meals include raw fish.*

read (reed)
1. to look at words and understand their meaning.
2. to say aloud written or printed words.

real (REE-ul, reel)
true; not false.

reason (REE-suhn)
why something is or should be a particular way.

record (REK-urd)
1. a round, flat, usually black piece of plastic with
  ridges that can make music on a record player.
2. a piece of writing about the past.
3. the very best performance. *The runner set a new
  world record.*

record (rih-KORD)
to make a tape or written entry of something. *The
  band will record again in March.*

rectangle (REK-tang-gul)
a four-sided shape with four equal angles.

reflect (rih-FLEKT)
to throw back light or heat.

refrigerator (rih-FRIJ-uh-RAY-tur)
a special container for keeping food cold and fresh.

refrigerator

region (REE-jun)
a large area of land.

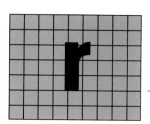

reindeer (RAYN-deer)
a large kind of deer with antlers that lives in cold
  northern lands.

relate (rih-LAYT)
1. to talk or write about. *The teacher asked us to relate
   the main causes of World War One.*
2. to show how things are joined together in some way.
   *Can you relate the flood to the melting snows in the
   mountains?*

reindeer

relative (REL-uh-tiv)
a person who is related to another by birth or
  marriage.

relax (rih-LAKS)
to stop worrying or working; to feel calm; to rest.

remember (rih-MEM-bur)
to store in the mind so you do not forget.

repair (rih-PAIR)
to mend; to fix.

report (rih-PORT)
1. to tell or write about something that has happened.
2. a written record that gives news.

reptile (REP-til, REP-tile)
a creature such as a snake or a lizard that is
  cold-blooded and has a scaly skin.

rescue (RES-kyoo)
to save someone who is in danger.

rest (rest)
1. to be still; to lie down; to sleep.
2. the others; whoever or whatever is left.

rescue

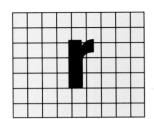

result (rih-ZULT)
how a thing ends. *The result of the game was a loss for our team.*

rhyme (rime)
1. to sound like another word, such as "tall" and "small."
2. a piece of poetry with lines that end in words sounding like each other, as in a nursery rhyme.

rhythm (RITH-um)
a steady pattern of sound or movement. *Music and poetry have rhythm.*

rice (rice)
a white or brown grain that is often cooked in water.

rice

rich (rich)
having a lot of money or goods.

ride (ride)
to sit or stand on something and be carried along.

right (rite)
1. correct.
2. the opposite of left.

ripe (ripe)
ready to use or eat, such as fruit at its best. *The tomatoes were big and ripe.*

river (RIV-ur)
a large stream of water that moves toward a lake or the sea.

road (rohd)
a hard, usually flat surface made for vehicles to travel along.

road

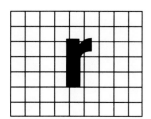

robber (ROB-ur)
a person who steals.

robot (ROH-but, ROH-baht)
a machine that can do different jobs, as a human being can; a machine made like a person.

rock (rok)
1. something hard that is made from one or more minerals.
2. to move backward and forward or from side to side.

rocket (ROK-it)
a tube with fuel in it that is shot into the air or into space.

rocks

rodeo (ROH-dee-OH, roh-DAY-oh)
a show or competition of cowboy skills.

roll (rol)
1. to move by turning over and over like a ball.
2. a list of names.
3. a kind of bread.

roof (roof)
the top covering of a building or vehicle.

rodeo

room (room)
1. one part of a building, such as a bedroom or a kitchen.
2. space to put something in. *There is no room in the box for any more toys.*

root (root)
the part of a plant under the ground that holds the plant in place and collects food and water from the earth.

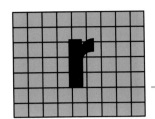

rope (rohp)
a thick, strong cord made by twisting thinner
  cords together.

rope

rough (ruf)
1. uneven; lumpy; not smooth.
2. wild; stormy. *The sea was rough today.*

round (round)
1. shaped like a ball.
2. the length of time boxers or wrestlers fight before
   they rest.

row (roh)
1. a line of things or people.
2. to move a boat through water by using two long
   paddles at the same time.

rub (rub)
to wipe hard, usually with a cloth or a brush.

rubber (RUB-ur)
the sap of the rubber tree and the stretchy material
  made from it.

rule (rool)
1. something said or written that points out how to act
   or behave.
2. to control; to be in charge of. *Who will rule if the
   queen dies?*

ruler (ROO-lur)
1. a straight piece of wood or metal used for
   measuring.
2. a man or woman who is the leader of a country.

ruler

run (run)
to move quickly.

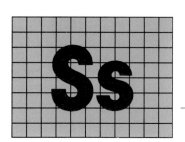

sad (sad)
feeling sorry; unhappy.

safe (sayf)
1. not in danger.
2. a very strong metal box for keeping money, jewelry,
   or other valuables locked away.

same (saym)
not different; exactly alike. *His boat is the same
   as mine.*

sand (sand)
1. rock that has been broken down into very, very
   small pieces.
2. to make something smooth by rubbing it.

sand

sandwich (SAND-wich, SAN-wich)
two pieces of bread with meat or some other food
   between them.

Saturday (SAT-ur-dee, SAT-ur-day)
the seventh day of the week.

save (sayv)
1. to keep something to use later.
2. to make safe; to help someone in danger; to rescue.

scare (skayr)
to frighten.

school (skool)
a place for teaching and learning.

school

science (SIGH-uns)
a way of learning about the earth and the universe by
   looking and testing very carefully.

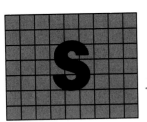

scissors (SIZ-urz)
a tool used for cutting that has two sharp blades
  fastened together in the middle.

scissors

scream (skreem)
a loud cry of fear, pain, or surprise.

seal (seel)
1. a large sea mammal that lives both in the ocean
  and on land and that eats fish.
2. to fasten something so that it cannot be opened
  without breaking the fastening.

season (SEE-zun)
1. a special time; usually one of four parts of the year.
  *As much as I like winter, spring, and summer, fall
  is the season I like best.*
2. to give more taste to food by adding something. *You
  should season that salad with vinegar.*

seat (seet)
something to sit on.

second (SEK-und)
1. next after first. *Susan came in second in the race.*
2. a very short time; one sixtieth of a minute. *It took
  just a second to open the door.*

secret (SEE-krit)
something known to only one or a few people.

see (see)
to use the eyes to look at something; to notice.

seed (seed)
the part of a plant from which a new plant will grow.

seeds

sell (sel)
to give something for money.

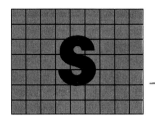

send (send)
to make a person or thing go somewhere.

separate (1. SEP-ur-it; 2. SEP-uh-RAYT)
1. not joined together; apart.
2. to go away from each other; to part.

September (Sep-TEM-bur)
the ninth month of the year; it has thirty days.

serious (SEER-ee-us)
important; not joking. *The look on the coach's face told the players he was serious.*

set (set)
a number of things of the same kind that belong together.

sew (soh)
to use a needle and thread to join cloth together.

sew

shadow (SHAD-oh)
the dark shape made by an object or person coming between a light and the ground or wall.

shake (shayk)
to move anything quickly from side to side or up and down.

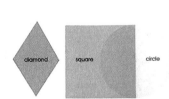

diamond   square   circle

shallow (SHAL-oh)
not deep; having very little distance from top to bottom. *The stream was so shallow that you could easily see the bottom.*

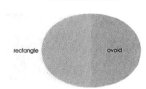

rectangle   ovoid

shape (shayp)
the form of a thing; the way something looks. *A ball is round in shape.*

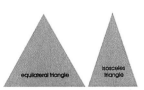

equilateral triangle   isosceles triangle

shapes

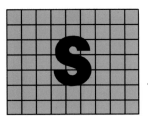
shark (shark)
a large, often dangerous ocean fish
  that has very sharp teeth.

sharp (sharp)
1. having an edge or tip that can cut. *The cat's
  claws are sharp.*
2. clever; fast in thinking. *Jean has a sharp mind for
  numbers.*

shark

sheep (sheep)
an animal whose coat gives wool.

sheet (sheet)
1. a large piece of cloth used to cover a bed.
2. a thin, flat piece of material, such as paper, glass,
  or metal.

shell (shel)
1. a hard outside covering, as on an egg or nut.
2. to take off the hard outside coverings of something.
  Could you shell some peanuts for me?

shells

shelter (SHEL-tur)
a place that keeps people, animals, or things safe
  from bad weather.

shine (shine)
1. to give out bright light. *The stars shine in the night sky.*
2. to polish. *Jane worked hard to shine the silver cup.*

ship (ship)
a large boat that sails across the oceans.

ships

shirt (shurt)
a piece of clothing made of cloth and worn on the
  upper part of the body.

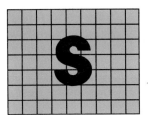

shoe (shoo)
a covering worn on the foot.

short (short)
1. not very long or very tall.
2. not lasting long.
3. not enough. *Mother was short of flour for baking.*

shovel (SHUV-ul)
a tool with a long handle and wide blade that is used
  for digging.

shovel

show (shoh)
1. to let someone see something. *I'll show you my
   stamp collection.*
2. to explain; to point out. *Peter can show me how to fry
   an egg.*

shower (SHOU-ur)
1. rain falling for only a short time.
2. to wash yourself while standing under a spray
   of water.

shrink (shringk)
to get smaller.

shut (shut)
1. closed; not open.
2. to close.

shut

sick (sik)
ill; not well or healthy.

sidewalk (SIDE-wok)
a hard, flat surface that people walk on and that is
  usually found alongside a street.

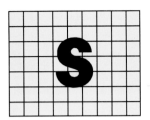

sign (sine)
1. to write your name on something. *Please sign this check.*
2. a notice that tells something. *Because of the fog, we missed the sign for the road exit.*

sign

silver (SIL-vur)
a shiny, gray-white, valuable metal.

sing (sing)
to use the voice to make music.

sit (sit)
to rest on a chair or some other seat.

size (size)
the space a thing takes up; how big or small something is.

skeleton (SKEL-ih-tun)
all the bones in the body.

skin (skin)
the outside covering of a fruit or of an animal's body.

skirt (skurt)
clothing that hangs down loosely from the waist over the legs; the part of a dress hanging from the waist.

sky (sky)
the space above the earth where clouds, the sun, the moon, and stars can be seen.

sleep (sleep)
a time of rest for the body and mind.

slice (slice)
a flat piece cut from something. *Will you have a slice of bread?*

slice

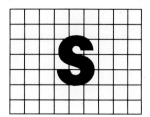

slide (slide)
to move very easily over a smooth surface.

slow (sloh)
1. not fast; taking a long time.
2. behind the time. *Fred's watch is five minutes slow.*

small (smawl)
not large.

smell (smehl)
1. what your nose tells you about something. *The smell of the skunk was what drove off the dog.*
2. to give out a smell. *These flowers smell sweet.*

smile (smile)
a happy look.

smoke (smohk)
the cloud that rises from something burning.

smooth (smooth)
level; without any bumps.

snake (snayk)
a crawling reptile with a long body and no legs.

snake

sneeze (sneez)
the sudden blowing noise made when something tickles the nose.

snow (snoh)
soft, white flakes of frozen water that fall from the sky.

soap (sohp)
a solid or liquid used with water to make things clean. *Plenty of soap should get out the dirt.*

snow

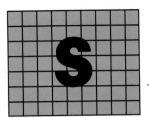

soft (soft)
1. not hard. *The sweater was very soft.*
2. gentle. *His voice was so soft that I could hardly hear him.*

soil (soyl)
1. the top part of the ground where plants grow; dirt.
2. to get something dirty. *Playing in the garden might soil your clothes.*

soldier (SOHL-jur)
an active member of an army.

solid (SOL-id)
having a firm, hard shape and size; not a liquid or gas.

song (song)
words and music together.

sour (sour)
not sweet to taste. *Lemons are sour.*

south (south)
one of the four main compass points; the opposite of north.

space (spays)
1. the distance between things.
2. a place with nothing in it.
3. the place far above the earth where there is no air.

speak (speek)
to say something.

special (SPESH-ul)
not common; different from others. *The special sale was only for one day.*

soldier

106

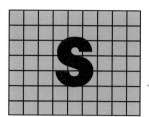

speed (speed)
the rate at which something moves. *The airplane landed at low speed.*

spell (spel)
1. to write or say the letters of a word in the right order.
2. words that are supposed to have magic power.

spend (spend)
to pay out money; to buy things.

spider (SPY-dur)
a small animal with four pairs of long legs that spins a web to catch insects for food.

spider

spoil (spoyl)
1. to damage something.
2. to become not fit for eating or drinking. *If you don't want the milk to spoil, put it in the refrigerator.*

spoon (spoon)
a tool with a handle and a shallow bowl that is used for eating or stirring liquids or soft food.

sport (sport)
a game such as football, fishing, tennis, and swimming.

spread (spred)
1. to cover. *Mary spread the jelly on her toast.*
2. to stretch out. *The bird spread its wings and flew off.*

sport

spring (spring)
1. the season of the year between winter and summer.
2. to move quickly up and down.
3. a place where water flows out of the earth.

spy (spy)
a person who secretly watches others.

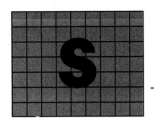

square (skwair)
1. a shape that has four straight sides with all the sides the same length.
2. an open place in a town.
3. to multiply a number by itself. *If you square 2, you'll get 4.*

square

stage (stayj)
a raised platform in a theater or hall.

stairs (stairz)
steps for walking up or down.

stamp (stamp)
1. the small piece of paper you lick and press onto an envelope or package to mail it.
2. to bang a foot or hoof on the ground. *The horse would always stamp if it wanted more hay.*

stamp

stand (stand)
to be on your feet.

start (start)
to begin. *When is the movie supposed to start?*

station (STAY-shun)
1. a place where trains or buses start from and stop.
2. a building for police and firefighters.

steady (STED-ee)
1. firm in position or place. *The apples rolled off the cart because it was not steady.*
2. staying the same. *Dave's father drove on the highway at a steady speed of fifty-five miles an hour.*

steal (steel)
to take something that belongs to someone else without that person knowing about it.

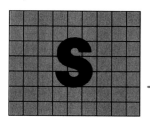

steam (steem)
1. the white cloud that comes from boiling water.
2. to cook by putting food over, but not in, boiling water.

steel (steel)
a strong metal made from iron.

steep (steep)
sloping very sharply. *The boys climbed the steep hill.*

steel

steer (steer)
to guide anything.

step (step)
1. a forward, backward, or side movement of the foot. *With every step on the ice, I thought I was going to fall.*
2. one of a series of raised surfaces, usually made of wood, stone, or metal. *The top step of the ladder was broken.*
3. one in a series of things to do; an act or action. *The first step of the project was easier than the second step.*

stick (stik)
1. a long, thin piece of wood.
2. anything shaped like a stick. *Peter bought a stick of gum.*
3. to fasten together with glue or paste.

stick

stiff (stif)
hard; firm; not easy to bend or move.

sting (sting)
a stab into the skin by an insect, animal, or plant. *A wasp sting is painful.*

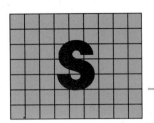

stir (stur)
to mix something.

stone (stohn)
1. a small rock.
2. a large, hard seed in the middle of some kinds of fruit, such as the plum and peach.

stop (stop)
1. to finish what you are doing.
2. the opposite of go.

store (stor)
1. a place where things are sold.
2. to put a thing away until it is needed.

store

storm (storm)
very bad weather with rain or snow, strong winds, and maybe thunder and lightning.

story (STOR-ee)
a tale that can be either true or made up.

straight (strayt)
without a bend or curve. *A ruler helps you draw a straight line.*

stranger (STRAYN-jur)
someone not known. *The man in the red hat is a stranger in town.*

stretch (strech)
to make something longer or wider by pulling.

strong (strong)
able to carry or lift heavy things; powerful.

student (STU-dunt)
a person who goes to school to learn.

student

110

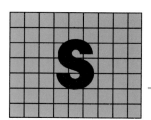

sudden (SUD-un)
happening quickly; not expected. *The branch broke with a sudden crack.*

sugar (SHUG-ur)
a food added to other foods and drinks to make them sweet.

summer (SUM-ur)
one of the four seasons of the year, coming between spring and autumn.

sun (sun)
the brightest object in the daytime sky, sending light and heat to the earth.

sun

Sunday (SUN-dee, SUN-day)
the first day of the week.

sure (shoor)
knowing that you are right; certain.

surprise (sur-PRIZE)
something that is not expected.

sweater

sweater (SWET-ur)
a heavy, knitted shirt.

sweet (sweet)
having a taste like sugar; the opposite of sour.

swim (swim)
to move on or in the water by moving the body.

swing (swing)
1. a seat hanging from ropes or chains.
2. to move back and forth.

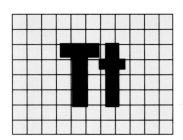

table (TAY-bul)
a piece of furniture with legs and a flat top.

tadpole (TAD-pohl)
a young frog or toad just hatched out of its egg.

tadpoles

tail (tayl)
the part at the end of something. *The monkey wrapped its tail around the branch and swung from it.*

talk (tawk)
to speak.

tall (tawl)
very high. *The giraffe is a tall animal.*

tame (taym)
not wild; friendly.

tap (tap)
to hit something gently.

tape (tayp)
1. a narrow strip of cloth, plastic, metal, or some other material that often has one sticky side. *We'll need more tape to put up these posters.*
2. to copy sounds or pictures on a special machine for this. *Did you tape last night's TV show?*

tape

taste (tayst)
to sense the flavor of something with the mouth. *You can taste the lime in the soda.*

tea (tee)
a drink made from the dried leaves of a plant that grows mainly in eastern Asia.

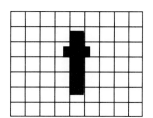

teach (teech)
to show someone how to do something; to give
  lessons. *Mr. Martin will teach you how to swim.*

teacher (TEECH-ur)
a person who teaches.

team (teem)
a number of people or animals working or playing
  together. *The team of dogs pulled the sled.*

tear (tair; rhymes with "air")
to rip; to pull apart.

tear (teer; rhymes with "ear")
one of the drops of water falling from the eyes
  when someone cries.

telephone (TEL-uh-FOHN)
an instrument that carries the voice so that you can
  speak with someone far away.

telephone

television (TEL-uh-VIZH-un)
an electrical instrument that brings sound and pictures
  over a wire or through the air from long distances.

tell (tel)
to say; to give news of something that has happened.

temperature (TEM-pur-uh-chur, TEM-pruh-chur)
the measure of how hot or cold something is.

tennis (TEN-is)
a game for two or four people, in which a ball is hit
  with rackets back and forth over a net.

tent (tent)
a small shelter made of cloth or canvas.

tent

113

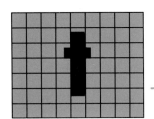

test (test)
1. a set of questions to see how much a person knows.
2. to find out whether something works properly. *The plumber began to test the pipe to see if it leaked.*

thaw (thaw)
the change from cold to warmer weather that melts snow or ice.

theater (THEE-uh-tur)
a building where people watch movies or plays.

thick (thik)
1. measured from one surface or side to the other; wide; not thin. *The walls are two feet thick.*
2. not flowing easily. *Syrup is a thick liquid.*

thief (theef)
someone who steals.

thin (thin)
not wide or fat. *A sheet of paper is very thin.*

think (thingk)
to use the mind.

thirsty (THUR-stee)
wanting a drink.

thread (thred)
a thin string made of many fibers twisted together.

thread

throw (throh)
to send something from the hand into the air.

thumb (thum)
the short, thick finger nearest to the wrist.

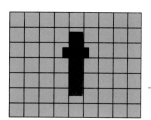

thunder (THUN-dur)
the loud noise heard after a flash of lightning in a storm.

Thursday (THURZ-dee, THURZ-day)
the fifth day of the week.

ticket (TIK-it)
a small piece of cardboard or paper to show
that someone has paid to do something. *I bought a
ticket to see the movie.*

ticket

tickle (TIK-ul)
1. a feeling on the surface of the skin that makes you
want to rub it.
2. a feeling in the nose that makes you want to sneeze.

tidy (TIE-dee)
neat; clean.

tie (tie)
1. to fasten with string or ribbon.
2. a narrow piece of cloth worn knotted
around the neck under a collar.
3. to come out equal in a game.

tiger (TIE-gur)
a big, fierce cat with orange-yellow
fur and black stripes that lives in Asia.

tight (tite)
fitting closely; not loose. *These shoes are so tight that
they hurt me.*

tiger

timber (TIM-bur)
1. living trees.
2. wood cut from trees that is used in building or in
making furniture.

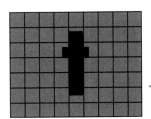

time (time)
1. the hour of the day shown on a clock.
2. seconds, minutes, hours, days, weeks, months, and years.
3. to measure how long it takes someone to do something.

tiny (TIE-nee)
very small.

tire (tire)
a strong rubber ring, usually filled with air, that fits around the outside of a wheel.

tire

title (TIE-tul)
1. the name of something. *No one could remember the title of the writer's last book.*
2. a name that points out position, rank, or something else about a person. *The young boy had the title of prince.*
3. what you have as long as you are champion. *Joe Louis held his world boxing title for many years.*

today (tuh-DAY)
this day; the present time.

toe (toh)
one of the five end parts of the foot.

tomorrow (tuh-MOR-oh)
the day after today.

toes

ton (tun)
a weight of 2,000 pounds, or 900 kilograms.

tongue (tung)
the thick, movable part in the mouth used for talking and eating.

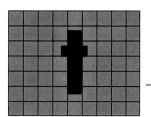

tonight (tuh-NITE)
this night.

tool (tool)
something that helps a person do work.

tooth (tooth)
one of the white bones in the mouth used for biting
and chewing.

tools

top (top)
1. the highest part of something.
2. a toy that spins.

torch (torch)
a flaming stick carried in the hand and used as a light.

touch (tuch)
1. to feel something with the fingers, hand, or some
   other part of the body.
2. to be so near that there is no space between. *The
   trees touch the side of our garage.*

tough (tuf)
1. hard; not easily broken. *We could not eat the tough
   meat.*
2. strong and brave.

town (toun)
a large number of houses and other buildings
together.

toy (toy)
something that children play with.

toy

traffic (TRAF-ik)
everything that moves by road, by sea, or by air.

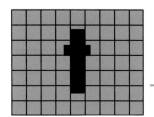

train (trayn)
1. a number of coaches or cars joined together and
   pulled by an engine on a railroad.
2. to teach.
3. to practice.

transparent (trans-PAR-ent)
clear; easy to see through.

transport (trans-PORT)
to carry something from one place to another.

train

trap (trap)
1. something used to capture an animal.
2. to capture.

travel (TRAV-ul)
to go from one place to another; to take a journey.

tree (tree)
a very large plant with a trunk, branches, and leaves.

triangle (TRY-ang-gul)
a shape with three straight sides and three angles.

truck (truk)
a motor vehicle for carrying heavy loads.

true (troo)
correct; real; the opposite of false. *Everything that
she told the police was true.*

trust (trust)
knowing or believing that someone says true things
and would not hurt you.

tree

truth (trooth)
something true and honest; opposite of lie.

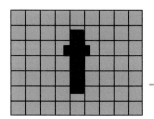

truthful (TROOTH-ful)
honest; not lying.

try (try)
to do the best you can.

T-shirt (TEE-shirt)
a light shirt with short sleeves that is pulled on over
  the head.

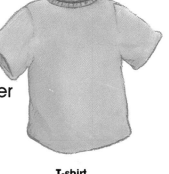
T-shirt

tube (toob, tyoob)
1. something that is long and hollow.
2. a plastic or soft-metal container from which the
  contents can be squeezed. *The tube of glue is empty.*

Tuesday (TOOZ-dee, TOOZ-day, TYOOZ-dee,
TYOOZ-day)
the third day of the week.

tunnel (TUN-el)
a passage cut through a hill or under the ground.

turkey (TUR-kee)
a large bird with thick feathers that lives in
  North America.

turkey

turn (turn)
1. to move left or right, or all the way around.
2. a chance. *It will soon be your turn to ride the pony.*

twin (twin)
one of two children or animals born at the same time
  to the same mother.

twist (twist)
to turn two or more things together, or turn something
  around and around. *Twist the threads to make
  a rope.*

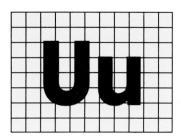

Uu

ugly (UG-lee)
not pretty; the opposite of beautiful.

umbrella (um-BREL-luh)
a frame of light metal covered by cloth that keeps out
the rain or sun.

umbrella

uncomfortable (un-KUM-furt-uh-bul,
un-KUMF-ter-bul)
not feeling happy or at ease.

understand (un-der-STAND)
to know what something means.

unhappy (un-HAP-pee)
sad; miserable.

unicorn (YOO-nih-korn)
an imaginary animal that looks like a horse with a horn
in the middle of its forehead.

unicorn

uniform (YOO-nih-form)
1. special clothes worn by people who belong to the
same group. *The soldier's uniform was blue.*
2. staying the same; not changing. *We traveled at
a uniform speed.*

universe (YOO-nih-vers)
everything that there is on earth and in space.

unkind (un-KIND)
cruel; not being good to others.

upset (up-SET)
to be unhappy or disappointed about something.

usual (YOO-zhoo-ul, YOO-zhwal)
almost always done; ordinary.

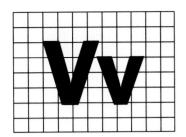

vacation (vay-KAY-shun; vuh-KAY-shun)
time spent away from work or school, for rest or fun.

valley (VAL-ee)
low ground between two mountains or hills.

valuable (VAL-yoo-uh-bul, VAL-yuh-bul)
worth much money; very important. *A diamond ring is valuable.*

vegetable (VEJ-tuh-bul, VEJ-ih-tuh-bul)
any plant other than a fruit or grain that is used for food.

vegetables

vehicle (VEE-ih-kul)
something used for carrying people and goods from place to place.

view (vyoo)
1. what one can see from a particular place.
2. to watch something.

visit (VIZ-it)
to go or come to see.

voice (voys)
the sound made when speaking and singing.

volcano (vol-KAY-noh)
a mountain that throws out hot ashes, melted rock, and steam through a hole at the top.

volcano

volume (VOL-yoom, VOL-yum)
1. a book. *There is only one volume left on my bookshelf.*
2. the amount of space something takes up. *Gallons and liters are measurements of liquid volume.*
3. how loud a sound is. *Please lower the volume of your radio.*

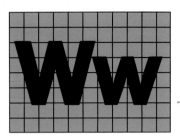

wag (wag)
to move quickly from side to side or up and down.

waist (wayst)
the middle part of the body between the chest and
  hips.

wait (wayt)
to stay in a place until something happens or
  someone comes.

wake (wayk)
to stop sleeping.

walk (wawk)
to move about on foot.

wall (wawl)
1. the solid sides of a building.
2. a brick or stone fence.

wall

war (wor)
a fight between countries or between groups of
  people in the same country.

warm (warm)
1. more hot than cold.
2. to heat. *Come by the fire and warm your hands.*

warning (WOR-ning)
what is said or written to stop people from doing
  something or to help them know something ahead
  of time. *"No swimming" was the warning on the sign
  near the fast-moving river.*

wash (wash)
to make clean with water or some other liquid.

wash

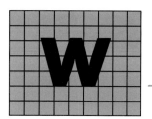

W

wasp (wasp)
a flying insect that stings.

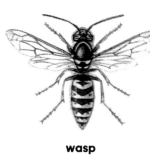

wasp

waste (wayst)
1. to use or spend something poorly or badly; to use something up. *Don't waste your money on that broken toy.*
2. something that is of little or no use; something thrown away. *Put all waste in the basket by the door.*

watch (wach)
1. a small clock usually worn on the wrist.
2. to look at something.
3. to guard.

water (WOT-ur)
1. the liquid in rivers, lakes, ponds, and oceans.
2. to wet with water. *Ruth is going to water the plants.*

wave (wayv)
1. a moving line of water on a lake or ocean.
2. to move up and down or from side to side. *Flags wave in the wind.*

weak (week)
having little strength or power.

weapon (WEP-un)
anything used for fighting or hunting. *A gun is a weapon.*

wear (wayr)
to have clothes on the body.

weather (WETH-ur)
how wet, dry, hot, or cold the air is outside.

web (web)
a kind of net that spiders make to catch insects.

web

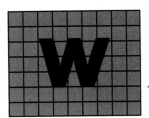

webbed (webd)
with a shape or pattern like a web. *A duck has webbed feet.*

Wednesday (WENZ-dee, WENZ-day)
the fourth day of the week.

weed (weed)
a plant that grows where it is not wanted in gardens, fields, and lawns.

week (week)
seven days.

weigh (way)
to find out how heavy something is.

west

west (west)
one of the four main compass points; the opposite of east.

wet (wet)
covered with water or another liquid; not dry. *Her coat was still wet with rain.*

whale (hwayl, wayl)
a huge mammal that lives in the ocean.

wheat (hweet, weet)
a plant whose grains are used to make flour.

whale

wheel (hweel, weel)
a circle of metal or wood, sometimes with a tire around it, that turns and helps things move easily.

whisper (HWIS-pur, WIS-pur)
to talk in a very soft voice.

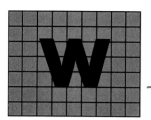

wicked (WIK-id)
very bad.

wide (wide)
stretching a long way from one side to the other;
  not narrow.

wild (wild)
not controlled by people; not tame. *Giraffes and lions
  are wild animals of Africa.*

win (win)
to be first in a game, race, or competition. *I think
  Julie will win the prize for the best writing.*

win

wind (wihnd; rhymes with "pinned")
air that moves quickly. *The strong wind blew the
  leaves off the trees.*

wind (wind; rhymes with "kind")
1. to twist or wrap. *Wind the string around your finger.*
2. to turn something on an object to make it work or to
  correct it. *Wind the clock back an hour.*

window (WIN-doh)
an opening, usually covered in glass, for seeing
  through.

wing (wing)
the part of a bird, insect, or airplane that helps keep it
  up when flying.

winter (WIN-tur)
the season between fall and spring; usually the
  coldest of the four seasons.

wings

wish (wish)
to want something very much.

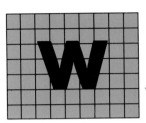

witch (wich)
a woman who is supposed to make magic. *The witch turned the prince into a frog.*

wizard (WIZ-urd)
a man who is supposed to make magic.

woman (WUM-un)
a lady; a female; a girl when grown up.

wonder (WUN-der)
1. something surprising or not usual. *The Grand Canyon is a wonder of nature.*
2. to want to know or learn. *I wonder how fish breathe.*

wood (wood)
1. the part of a tree under the bark.
2. a place where many trees grow.

wool (wul)
the soft, thick hair of sheep and lambs that is used to make clothes and other things.

wool

work (wurk)
1. something done for pay or for a living; a job.
2. to be in action; to run something, such as a machine. *Can you work the computer?*

world (wurld)
1. the earth.
2. the universe.
3. a planet.

worm (wurm)
a small animal that has soft skin, lives underground, and crawls.

worm

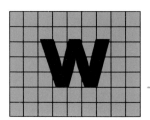

worry (WUR-ee)
to be uneasy; to be uncomfortable in the mind. *My parents worry if I am late.*

worth (wurth)
1. good value.
2. something useful or enjoyable.

wound (woond)
1. a cut in someone's flesh.
2. to injure or hurt.

wrap (rap)
1. to cover something with paper. *Wrap the gifts before Monica sees them.*
2. to wind, twist, or fold something around. *Wrap that pipe with tape.*

wrap

wrench (rench)
1. to pull or twist with a hard, sharp motion. *She tried to wrench the ball from his hands.*
2. a tool with jaws that is used to grip and turn a bolt or nut.

write (rite)
to draw letters, words, and figures so that people can read them.

writing (RITE-ing)
something that has been put down in letters and words.

wrong (rong)
1. not right or good. *It is wrong to steal and to lie.*
2. not true; not correct. *Many of your answers are wrong.*

write

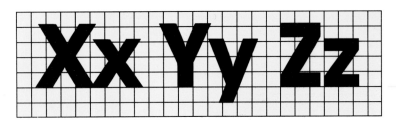

Xx Yy Zz

x ray (EKS-ray)
a picture made by a special machine that shows the inside of a body.

x ray

yard (yard)
1. an area of ground around a house.
2. a length of three feet, or thirty-six inches (ninety-one centimeters).

yawn (yawn)
to open the mouth wide and breathe in and out, especially when you're sleepy or bored.

year (yeer)
a period of 12 months, 52 weeks, or 365 days; the time it takes the earth to go once around the sun.

yesterday (YES-tur-dee, YES-tur-day)
the day before today.

young (yung)
in the early part of life; the opposite of old.

zebra (ZEE-bruh)
an African animal that looks like a horse with stripes.

Zip Code (ZIP KOHD)
the numbers placed at the end of an address to help the post office sort the mail.

zipper (ZIP-ur)
a metal or plastic fastener that slides up and down. *Mother took the buttons off the coat and put on a zipper.*

zebra

zoo (zoo)
a place where people can safely see many different kinds of wild animals.